SAMMY FRANCO

HEAVY BAG BIBLE

3 BEST-SELLING HEAVY BAG BOOKS IN ONE MASSIVE COLLECTION

Also by Sammy Franco

Double End Bag Workout
Bruce Lee's 5 Methods of Attack
The Widow Maker Compendium
Invincible: Mental Toughness Techniques for Peak Performance
Unleash Hell: A Step-by-Step Guide to Devastating Widow Maker Combinations
Feral Fighting: Advanced Widow Maker Fighting Techniques
The Widow Maker Program: Extreme Self-Defense for Deadly Force Situations
Savage Street Fighting: Tactical Savagery as a Last Resort
Heavy Bag Workout
Heavy Bag Combinations
Heavy Bag Training
The Complete Body Opponent Bag Book
Stand and Deliver: A Street Warrior's Guide to Tactical Combat Stances
Maximum Damage: Hidden Secrets Behind Brutal Fighting Combinations
First Strike: End a Fight in Ten Seconds or Less!
The Bigger They Are, The Harder They Fall
Self-Defense Tips and Tricks
Kubotan Power: Quick & Simple Steps to Mastering the Kubotan Keychain
Gun Safety: For Home Defense and Concealed Carry
Out of the Cage: A Guide to Beating a Mixed Martial Artist on the Street
Warrior Wisdom: Inspiring Ideas from the World's Greatest Warriors
War Machine: How to Transform Yourself Into a Vicious and Deadly Street Fighter
1001 Street Fighting Secrets
When Seconds Count: Self-Defense for the Real World
Killer Instinct: Unarmed Combat for Street Survival
Street Lethal: Unarmed Urban Combat

Heavy Bag Bible: Three Best-Selling Heavy Bag Books in One Massive Collection (Books 1-3)
Copyright © 2015 by Sammy Franco
ISBN: 978-1-941845-21-9
Printed in the United States of America
Published by Contemporary Fighting Arts, LLC.
Visit us Online at: **SammyFranco.com**
Follow us on Twitter: **@RealSammyFranco**

All rights reserved. Except for use in a review, no portion of this book may be reproduced in any form without the express written permission of the author. Direct inquiries and/or orders to the above address.

For author interviews or publicity information, please send inquiries in care of the publisher.

Table of Contents

Preface	VI
Book One: Heavy Bag Training	1
Book Two: Heavy Bag Combinations	131
Book Three: Heavy Bag Workouts	325
Heavy Bag Resources	479
Appendix	481
Glossary of Terms	493
About Sammy Franco	523

"Punch until you can't punch anymore, then punch some more."
— *Sammy Franco*

Warning!

The self-defense techniques, tactics, methods, and information described and depicted in this book can be dangerous and could result in serious injury and or death and should not be used or practiced in any way without the guidance of a professional reality based self-defense instructor.

The author, publisher, and distributors of this book disclaim any liability from loss, injury, or damage, personal or otherwise, resulting from the information and procedures in this book. ***This book is for academic study only.***

Before you begin any exercise program, including those suggested in this book, it is important to check with your physician to see if you have any condition that might be aggravated by strenuous exercise.

Preface

The Heavy Bag Bible includes my three best-selling heavy bag books collected into one huge paperback collection. This massive 570+ page book contains the entire Heavy Bag Training Series (Books 1-3).

Book One is **Heavy Bag Training,** and it introduces you to the foundational knowledge and skills necessary to maximize your heavy bag workouts. In this information-packed book, you'll find the important answers to the many questions about heavy bag training.

Heavy Bag Combinations is the second book in the training series. This unique book is your ultimate guide to mastering devastating heavy bag punching combinations. Many experienced fighters will find these punching combinations exceptionally challenging. However, the best feature of this book is that it teaches you how to create an unlimited number of heavy bag workout programs filled with an infinite amount of unique punching combinations.

Book Three is **Heavy Bag Workout**, and it features over two dozen *out of the box* workout routines that will maximize your fighting skills for boxing, mixed martial arts, kickboxing, self-defense, and personal fitness. Heavy Bag Workout has beginner, intermediate and advanced workout routines that will improve your speed, power, timing, endurance, and explosiveness. Whether you're an elite fighter or a complete beginner, this comprehensive book will take your fighting skills to the next level and beyond!

The heavy bag techniques featured in this massive book are based on my 30+ years of research, training and teaching the martial arts and combat sciences. I have taught these unique training methodologies to thousands of students, and I'm confident they will help you achieve higher levels of training performance.

Practitioners who regularly use this massive training guide as a reference tool will quickly improve their heavy bag skills. In fact, the information featured in this oversized book will dramatically improve your fighting skills, condition your body, and breathe new life into your current heavy bag program.

Finally, I strongly recommend that you read each book from beginning to end, chapter by chapter. Only after you have read all three books should you treat it as a reference and skip around, reading those chapters or subjects that interest you.

Train Hard!

- Sammy Franco

VIII

HEAVY BAG TRAINING

For Boxing, Mixed Martial Arts and Self-Defense

BOOK 1 OF A CONTINUING SERIES

SAMMY FRANCO

"Take things as they are. Punch when you have to punch. Kick when you have to kick."

- Bruce Lee

Contents

About this book … 5

Chapter 1: The Heavy Bag … 7

Chapter 2: Getting Started … 21

Chapter 3: The Fighting Stance and Footwork … 45

Chapter 4: How to Punch Correctly … 59

Chapter 5: Heavy Bag Techniques … 73

Chapter 6: Heavy Bag Workouts … 105

Caution!

The author, publisher, and distributors of this book disclaim any liability from loss, injury, or damage, personal or otherwise, resulting from the information and procedures in this book. This book is for academic study only.

The information contained in this book is not designed to diagnose, treat, or manage any physical health conditions.

Before you begin any exercise or activity, including those suggested in this book, it is important to check with your physician to see if you have any condition that might be aggravated by strenuous training.

Book One: Heavy Bag Training

About this book

Heavy Bag Training is my first book in the Heavy Bag Training Series. Practitioners who use this text as a reference tool will establish a rock solid foundation for heavy bag training. In fact, the skills and techniques featured in this book will significantly improve your fighting skills, enhance your conditioning, and introduce you to new aspects of heavy bag training.

The skills and techniques featured in this book will also help you achieve maximum training performance in a variety of professional and recreational activities including, boxing, mixed martial arts, martial arts (traditional and eclectic) kickboxing, self-defense, and personal fitness.

This introductory book covers a broad range of heavy bag skills that will allow to maximize your workouts. In this information-packed guide, you'll find answers to the most important questions about heavy bag training.

All of information and knowledge featured in this book are based on my 30+ years of research, training and teaching the martial arts and combat sciences. I have taught these unique skills to thousands of my students, and I'm confident they will help you reach higher levels of training performance.

Heavy Bag Training has six chapters, each one covers a critical aspect of training. In addition, you will also find a glossary of terms at the end of the book. Since this is both a skill-building workbook and training guide, feel free to write in the margins, underline passages, and dog-ear the pages.

Finally, I encourage you to read this book from beginning to end, chapter by chapter. Only after you have read the entire book should you treat it as a reference and skip around, reading those chapters or combinations that directly apply to you.

Train hard!

- Sammy Franco

Book One: Heavy Bag Training

Chapter 1
The Heavy Bag

The Oldest Piece of Training Equipment?

The heavy bag is, without a doubt, one of the oldest and most recognizable pieces of training equipment. However, with so many different types of bags on the market, it becomes confusing and sometimes overwhelming for the consumer. In many cases, they end up purchasing the wrong type of heavy bag for their training needs.

The heavy bag is a cylindrical shaped bag designed to be repeatedly kicked, punched and struck by the practitioner. Most traditional heavy bags are 14 inches in diameter and 42 inches in length. The interior of the bag is usually filled with either cotton fiber, thick foam, sand or other durable material. However, there are some heavy bags that can be filled with water (often called "water bags") which provide a more realistic target feel for the practitioner.

The exterior of the heavy bag can be constructed with a variety of different materials. For example, the least expensive bags are usually made of heavy canvas or vinyl while more expensive types are made of thick leather.

Depending on the brand, heavy bags can weigh anywhere from seventy-five to two hundred and fifty pounds. However, the average bag will weigh approximately eighty-five pounds.

Keep in mind, a quality punching bag is designed to take a tremendous amount of punishment and should absorb the most powerful of blows.

Since heavy bags are so popular, you can find just about every type of bag by simply surfing the Internet. However, be prepared, it can be a bit overwhelming as there are so many on the market.

So Many Different Bags to Choose From

The heavy bag is just one of many types of punching bags on the market. For example, punching bags may also include the body

Book One: Heavy Bag Training

Pictured here, the traditional heavy bag.

The heavy bag is, without a doubt, one of the oldest and most recognizable pieces of training equipment.

Heavy Bag Bible

opponent bag (BOB), double-end bag, speed bag, uppercut bag, body snatcher bag as well as many others. This book, however, is going to focus exclusively on the traditional heavy bag.

The heavy bag is the single most important piece of training equipment for boxing, mixed martial arts, self-defense as well as many styles of martial arts. The primary purpose of the punching bag is to develop power in all of your offensive "striking" techniques (e.g. jabs, crosses, hooks, uppercuts, elbow and knee strikes, etc.).

The body opponent bag is ideal for specialized self-defense training like razing skills, first strike scenarios, choking techniques and even stick fighting training. However, when it comes to developing actual punching power, the BOB is a poor choice. The head of the body opponent bag is too light and flimsy and cannot withstand the impact of power punching. It just does not offer the necessary resistance for the practitioner.

Did you know that the legendary Bruce Lee used to work out on a 300-pound heavy bag?

Book One: Heavy Bag Training

"Heavy Bag" is a popular term that may erroneously refer to a broad range of punching bags. For example, don't confuse the heavy bag with its cousin, the double-end bag that is used for developing speed, timing, and fighting reflexes. These light bags are useful and do have their purpose, but they don't hold a candle to the superior heavy bag. In this photo, the author performs a horizontal elbow strike on the double end bag.

Buying a Heavy Bag

When looking to buy a heavy bag, avoid purchasing it from your local sporting goods store, as most of these bags are cheap, poorly made and won't provide years of reliable use. The heavy bag is a serious piece of training equipment, so you should spare no expense and look for the highest quality brand that you can afford. Not only will it provide years of reliable use, but it will help ensure a better workout.

Again, you can find a reasonably priced quality bag on the

Book One: Heavy Bag Training

Internet. Here are just a few reputable companies:

- Ringside Equipment (**ringside.com**)
- Combat Sports, Inc (**combatsports.com**)
- Title Boxing (**titleboxing.com**)
- Amazon.com (amazon.com)

The actual weight of the bag is another important consideration when making a purchase. As a rule of thumb, try to buy the heaviest bag you can afford. Remember, when it comes to heavy bag training, *the heavier, the better!* If possible, avoid buying a bag that weighs under 100 pounds. Anything lighter will provide insufficient resistance causing the bag to swing uncontrollably when working out. I use a 150-pound heavy bag in my training and it offers me the perfect amount of resistance for intense power punching sessions.

If possible, avoid purchasing a self-standing punching bag. While these bags might look like a heavy bag, I can assure you they are not. In fact, these bags are poorly designed and cannot withstand the impact power of a heavy hitter.

Benefits of Heavy Bag Training

The heavy bag is a fantastic piece of training equipment that provides a full range of benefits for the practitioner. In this section, I am going to discuss some of the many benefits that come from working out on the bag.

Cardiovascular Conditioning

If you workout on the heavy bag with a significant amount of intensity, you can turn it into a challenging cardiovascular workout. However, this will require you to push yourself and throw your punches, kicks and strikes at a very respectable pace. Keep in mind, if you deliver your blows maximum power and intensity, your workout will quickly become an anaerobic workout, and you'll most likely fizzle out.

Heavy bag sessions can last anywhere from 30 seconds to 5 minutes depending on your level of conditioning, personal goals and training objectives. Much more is discussed in Chapter 6.

Improving Muscle Tone

Heavy bag training can also improve the muscle tone in your entire body including your back, chest, shoulders, arms, chest, abdominals, legs, and calves. A typical heavy bag workout can also burn a significant amount of calories and, therefore, can be a useful method for stripping fat from your body.

While heavy bag training does improve muscle tone, it should not be used as a substitute for weight training. For those of you who want to achieve noticeable strength gains, I strongly encourage a progressive resistance exercise program.

Book One: Heavy Bag Training

Martial artists, of all styles, use the heavy bag in their training. In this photo, a traditional Karateka delivers a reverse punch to the bag.

While regular heavy bag training will improve your muscle tone, it should not be used as a substitute for weight training.

Developing Fighting Technique

The heavy bag is also a fantastic piece of equipment for developing your fighting skills and techniques. It is no surprise that boxers, kickboxers, self-defense practitioners, MMA fighters, and martial artists of all styles and backgrounds regularly use the heavy bag for developing their particular style of fighting.

As you can imagine, a wide variety of kicks, punches and strikes can be developed and ultimately perfected on the heavy bag. Some techniques include:

- *Jab*
- *Lead straight punch*
- *Rear cross (also called a straight right)*
- *Hook punches*
- *Shovel hooks*
- *Uppercut*
- *Elbow strikes*
- *Knee strikes*
- *Kicking techniques*

The Heavy Bag is not just limited to stand-up fighting. It can also be used for ground fighting strikes. This is often referred to as "ground and pound" techniques.

Book One: Heavy Bag Training

Developing Fighting Attributes

Fighting attributes are unique qualities that enhance or amplify a particular fighting skill or technique. They might include speed, power, timing, agility, ambidexterity, coordination, combat conditioning as well as many others.

The heavy bag is an ideal piece of equipment for developing some of these fighting attributes. They include some of the following:

- *Impact power*
- *Ambidexterity*
- *Offensive timing*
- *Balance*
- *Eye/Hand coordination*
- *Footwork skills*
- *Non-telegraphic movement*
- *Muscular relaxation*

Heavy Bag Bible

- *Distancing*
- *Accuracy*

Fighting attributes are not just limited to the physical plane. In fact, there are mental and psychological attributes that can also be developed through consistent heavy bag training. They include:

- *Mental toughness*
- *Self-confidence*
- *Mental concentration*
- *Instrumental aggressiveness*
- *Immediate resilience*

Effective Stress Reduction Tool

There's no escaping the fact that mental stress can do a tremendous amount of damage by causing heart disease, high blood pressure, chest pain and an irregular heartbeat. It's no wonder stress is called the silent killer.

The good news is, working out on the heavy bag on a regular basis can be an excellent form of stress reduction. Punching and kicking an inanimate object, such as a heavy bag, permits you to channel pent-up aggression in a productive fashion.

Anger Management Tool

Unless you live on your own island, you will most likely live in a populated region that puts you in contact with many people every day. Add a hectic lifestyle to the mix and you will probably encounter occasional conflicts with difficult and belligerent people.

In such situations, you will sometimes get a sudden urge to respond in a physical manner, but as a law-abiding citizen, you must repress these primitive urges.

Working out on the heavy bag allows you to vent toxic anger in an acceptable and appropriate way. It's no wonder the heavy bag is one of the most recommended items for children and adults in therapy.

When used correctly, the heavy bag training can be a great stress reducing tool.

Inexpensive Investment

Finally, for the people on a tight budget, the good news is that heavy bag training is inexpensive. Essentially, all you need is a quality heavy bag and a good pair of bag gloves to protect your hands. Please see Chapter 2 to learn more about essential training gear.

Book One: Heavy Bag Training

Chapter 2
Getting Started

Finding the Right Place to Train

One of the most important considerations when setting up the heavy bag is finding the right location for working out. First, you will need a place that will allow both you and the bag to move around freely. The location should also be a relatively quiet place that is free of distractions. Here are a few places you might want to consider when setting up your bag:

- *Garage*
- *Carport*
- *Basement*
- *Barn*
- *Home gym (if you're fortunate enough)*
- *Open field or backyard*
- *Warehouse*
- *Under a deck*

If you can manage to clear out the clutter from your garage, it can be a perfect place for working out on the bag.

Book One: Heavy Bag Training

You can get somewhat creative when choosing a location to set up your heavy bag.

Heavy bag training outdoors is a great experience. However, exposing your bag to the elements, for a prolonged period, will quickly destroy your bag. Be sure to bring your bag indoors at the end of every workout.

Heavy Bag Bible

Hanging the Bag

Once you have found a suitable location to set up the bag, your next task is to hang it up. There are many different ways to hang the heavy bag, but the most important criterion is to attach the bag to a strong and stable structure that can withstand a tremendous amount of abuse.

Just about every heavy bag will come with four equal length chain links and either an "S" hook or snap link. To connect the chains to the bag, connect each one of the chain links to each of the metal rings attached to each corner of the bag. Then join the top of the chain links to the "S" hook or snap link above the bag.

Pictured here, a close-up of the four chain links that connect to the heavy bag. In some cases, you might have to cut or modify the chains to meet the requirements of your particular set up.

To reduce wear and tear on your link chains and to help give your bag a bit of a realistic bounce, I strongly recommend placing a heavy duty metal spring between the hanger and the top of the linked chains. Pictured here, a heavy duty metal spring.

Heavy Bag Hangers

Most people will find they can hang their heavy bag from either a wood or steel beam located in either their basement or garage. Luckily, there are several commercial heavy bag hangers that will allow you to hang your bag.

If, however, it's not possible to hang your bag from a beam, there are wall mount hangers that can be bolted into the wall studs.

Pictured here, a steel I-beam heavy bag hanger.

Heavy Bag Bible

Different Types of Heavy Bag Hangers

- *Steel I-Beam hanger*
- *Rafter hanger*
- *Wood Beam T-Swivel hanger*
- *Flat Wood Beam hanger*
- *Wall Mount hanger*
- Swing hanger

In this photo, a wall mounted heavy bag hanger.

Book One: Heavy Bag Training

The Heavy Bag Stand

Finally, if you do not have access to a solid beam or a wall stud but do have the space, you might want to consider investing in a heavy bag stand. These free-standing units are increasingly popular, as well as affordable. The only real drawback to a heavy bag stand is they limit your ability to move 360 degrees around the bag.

Like the wall mount hanger, the heavy bag stand will also limit your ability to move 360 degrees around the bag.

Setting the Proper Height of the Bag

Once you hang the heavy bag, the next important issue is making certain it is set at the proper height. One of the biggest mistakes people make is setting the height of the bag too low.

Be sure that your heavy bag is set up so that you can land headshots on the bag. This is especially important for people who intend on using the heavy bag for self-defense or sports combat like mixed martial arts. Essentially, the top of the heavy bag should be approximately 8-12 inches above your head.

In most cases, to ensure the proper height you might have to alter or cut the length of the chains that suspend the heavy bag. This will most likely take a bit of experimentation and some trial and error, but the result will be worth the effort.

Here's a good example of a heavy bag that is set up at the proper height. Notice how the top of the bag is well above the practitioner's head, yet it's not so high that it limits his ability to deliver body shots.

Book One: Heavy Bag Training

To ensure the proper height of the bag, make certain the top of the bag is approximately 8 to 12 inches taller than you. In this photo, notice how the heavy bag is hanging too low for this man. As a result, his ability to deliver punishing head shots will be significantly limited.

Heavy Bag Bible

Setting the proper height for the heavy bag also applies to the self-standing punching bag. In this photo, notice how the top of the bag is too low for this man. Once again, it should be approximately 8-12 inches taller than the practitioner.

This bag is too high for the practitioner. This mistake will limit your ability to deliver body and kicking techniques on the bag.

Book One: Heavy Bag Training

Heavy Bag Safety Tips

Before you launch ahead and start hitting the heavy bag, it's important to go over some important safety tips.

- Consult with your personal physician before beginning this or any other strenuous exercise program.
- Immediately stop training if you feel pain or discomfort.
- To avoid injuries, always begin your heavy bag workout with a light round first.
- Never hold your breath when working out on the bag.
- Always remember to exhale when delivering a blow to the bag.
- Always keep your workout area clear of objects.
- While punching or kicking the heavy bag, make certain that no one is standing near the bag. This includes pets.
- When setting up the heavy bag, always follow the manufacturer's instructions.
- Never workout on a canvas heavy bag without hand protection.
- To avoid hyper-extending your arm, never strike the bag unless you sure you will make contact.
- Always warm up with light stretching before working out on the bag.
- Never hang a heavy bag directly next to a window.
- Before you workout, always check and make certain the heavy bag and its support structure is secure.
- Immediately replace worn parts such as chain links, "S" hooks, snap links and other metal parts that wear out over time.
- When working out on the bag, always remember to keep both

Heavy Bag Bible

Pictured here, a heavy bag station at a Muay Thai kickboxing school.

Book One: Heavy Bag Training

of your hands up at all times.

- Always wear loose fitting clothing when working out on the bag.
- To avoid injuring your hands and damaging your bag, never workout with rings or jewelry on your hands.
- Never strike the heavy bag with full force until you have mastered the proper body mechanics.
- To avoid spraining or breaking your wrists, never bend your wrists when punching the bag.
- Don't strike the heavy bag with bare knuckles until your hands are conditioned to withstand the impact.
- Get into the habit of timing you workout rounds.
- Proper punching and kicking form is always more important than intensity.
- Never fully extend or "lock out" your arms when punching the bag.
- Depending on the type of punch or kick that you are executing, always maintain the correct distance from the bag.
- Never allow people to swing from the heavy bag.
- Avoid lifting your chin and exposing your centerline when working out on the bag.
- Maintain proper footwork and stay balanced at all times when working out on the bag.
- If your hands are sore from a previous heavy bag workout, consider wearing a pair of boxing gloves the next time you work out.

Heavy Bag Gear

If you want to get the most out of your workouts, you might want to invest in some heavy bag gear. While I did mention that heavy bag training is a relatively inexpensive activity, there are a few items you might want to consider purchasing to help you with your training.

Bag Gloves

One of the most important items to purchase for heavy bag training is a good pair of bag gloves. Bag gloves are lightweight gloves that offer excellent protection to your hands when working out on all types of punching bags.

Bag gloves are constructed of either top grain cowhide or durable vinyl. There are two styles of bag gloves sold on the market:

- *Mitt style gloves*
- *Finger style gloves*

Some of the mitt style bag gloves may also have a small metal bar sewn into the palm grip area to aid in fist stabilization. Bag glove sizes are usually small, medium, large and extra large.

When buying bag gloves, spare no expense and look for a reputable and high-quality brand. This will provide years of reliable use and will help ensure a better quality workout.

If you don't think you will need bag gloves, think again. Working out on the heavy bag, without hand protection causes sore knuckles, bruised bones, hand inflammation, sore wrists and bloody knuckles. More importantly, it will set your training back for several weeks for your hands to completely heal.

Book One: Heavy Bag Training

Pictured here, traditional mitt style bag gloves.

In this photo, finger style bag gloves.

Boxing Gloves

People often confuse bag gloves with boxing gloves. While the two might appear similar, they are quite different. Boxing gloves are heavier and significantly larger than bag gloves, and they are generally used for full-contact sparring and sports combat competition.

However, boxing gloves also can be used for heavy bag training. In fact, boxing gloves are often used by advanced practitioners for developing strength and endurance in their arms.

The ideal boxing glove is one that provides comfort, protection, and durability. Depending on your training objective, the glove can weigh anywhere from ten to sixteen ounces.

Here are some important features to be aware of when purchasing a pair of boxing gloves:

- To avoid wrist injuries, you want the glove to fit snugly around your hand.
- The boxing glove should be composed of multi-layered foam padding.

Book One: Heavy Bag Training

- The glove should have a sufficient palm grip that provides comfort and fist stabilization.
- To avoid a thumb injury, the glove should have thumb-lock stitching.
- The glove should be double-stitched to ensure durability.
- The entire glove should be constructed of top quality materials to increase its durability.
- The glove should be relatively easy to slip-on and off your hands. Velcro fasteners are sometimes preferred over laces.

As you can see, there's a big difference between the bag glove (right) and the boxing glove (left).

Boxing gloves can also be used if your knuckles are too sore or bruised to hit the heavy bag with regular bag gloves. The extra padding can make all the difference between skipping a workout and sticking with your routine.

Hand Wraps

Hand Wraps (also called wrist wraps) are used by experienced athletes who want an added measure of protection to their hands and wrists when hitting the heavy bag. They provide support to the entire hand and wrist area and can help prevent osteoarthritis in later years.

Essentially, hand wraps are long strips of cloth measuring two inches wide and nine to eighteen feet long. The longer hand wraps are more often used by practitioners who have large hands and who wish to have greater hand protection. You can find hand wraps at most sporting goods stores as well as the Internet.

Hand wraps should only be used in conjunction with either large bag gloves or boxing gloves, do not strike the heavy bag with just your hand wraps as this can easily injure your hands.

Hand wraps are washable and should be cleaned after every workout. Although there are many hand wrapping techniques, the procedures shown on page 40 is suggested.

While hand wraps are a necessary piece of training equipment for boxing, mixed martial arts and other competitive combat sports, I don't recommend using them for self-defense training. Reality based self-defense training requires you to condition your hands and wrists to withstand the impact of striking a solid target.

In professional combat sports, hand wraps are often used in conjunction with sports tape. However, most competitions will have specific rules regarding the amount and types of material you can use in competition.

Book One: Heavy Bag Training

A close-up view of hand wraps.

Heavy Bag Bible

How to Apply Hand and Wrist Wraps

How to wrap your hands and wrists with hand wraps. Follow steps A through P

Book One: Heavy Bag Training

Hand wraps are used all over the world and by many cultures. Here, a Muay Thai fighter takes a break during his training.

Heavy Bag Bible

Hand wraps should only be used with either large bag gloves or boxing gloves. Don't strike the bag with just your hand wraps, it will tear up your knuckles.

Never use weight lifting gloves for heavy bag training. These gloves provide no protection for your hands or wrists.

Interval Workout Timer

Since heavy bag training is structured around time and rounds, you should invest in a good workout timer. Boxers, mixed martial artists and kickboxers will use workout timers to keep track of their time during their rounds.

Most workout timers will allow you to adjust your round lengths anywhere from 30 seconds to 9 minutes. Rest time can be set from 30 seconds to 5 minutes depending on your level of conditioning and training goals.

There are several professional timers sold on the market, and they will vary in price. Your best bet is to search the Internet for one that meets your specific needs.

Workout Timers are great for:

- Keeping track of the number of rounds and the time of each round when working out alone.
- Measuring your current level of cardiovascular conditioning.
- Monitoring your progress in your heavy bag training.
- Creating healthy competition in your heavy bag routine.

One final reminder before moving on to the next chapter. Heavy bag training can be very demanding on the heart. Before you begin any workout program, including those suggested in this book, it is important to check with your physician to see if you have any condition that might be aggravated by strenuous exercise.

Book One: Heavy Bag Training

Chapter 3
The Fighting Stance and Footwork

Heavy Bag Bible

The Fighting Stance

Whether you are a boxer, mixed martial artist, street fighter or fitness junkie, you'll need to learn about the fighting stance.

The fighting stance is a strategic and aggressive posture you assume when squared-off with the heavy bag. For all intents and purposes, the fighting stance is the foundation for all of your punches and kicking techniques.

When working out on the heavy bag, the fighting stance will provide the following for the practitioner:

- Speed
- Striking power
- Stability when striking
- Mobility
- Balance
- Offensive fluidity
- Maximizes limb extension
- Complete visual picture

The fighting stance is not only used for working out. As a matter of fact, in actual combat the fighting stance is used for both offensive and

Book One: Heavy Bag Training

defensive purposes. It stresses strategic soundness and simplicity over complexity and style. The fighting stance also facilitates maximum execution of punches, kicks and strikes while simultaneously protecting your targets against possible counter attacks from the opponent.

The Centerline

One of the most important considerations of a fighting stance is the centerline. Your centerline is an imaginary vertical line that divides your body in half. Located on this line are some of your most vital impact targets. This includes your eyes, nose, chin, throat, solar plexus, and groin.

Centerline Placement

The proper placement of your centerline (in relation to the heavy bag) is critical and will directly effect the following:

1. Target Exposure - A properly positioned centerline will minimize the number of anatomical targets exposed to the bag when working out.

The Centerline

2. Balance - A properly positioned centerline will maximize your balance and stability during your workout. This is especially important when delivering explosive combination attacks.

3. Mobility - A properly positioned centerline will also maximize your ability to move quickly and efficiently around the bag.

4. Power Generation - A properly angled centerline permits

47

Heavy Bag Bible

maximum hip and shoulder rotation which translates to greater impact power when throwing punches, strikes, and other blows at the bag. For example, try throwing a punch at the bag with both of your feet planted squarely in front of you? Notice anything? There's no power, of course.

```
          ┌─────────────────┐
          │   Centerline    │
          │   Placement     │
          └────────┬────────┘
     ┌─────────────┼─────────────┐
┌────┴────┐   ┌────┴────┐   ┌────┴────┐
│ Target  │   │Balance &│   │  Power  │
│Exposure │   │ Mobility│   │Generation│
└─────────┘   └─────────┘   └─────────┘
```

Your centerline placement will have a direct effect on the following factors.

How To Assume a Fighting Stance

Essentially, there are two variations of the fighting stance, the orthodox and southpaw. Let's begin with the orthodox stance.

To assume the orthodox stance, place the left side of your body forward and closest to the heavy bag. Then, blade your feet and centerline at approximately forty-five degrees from your bag. Make certain to place your feet approximately a shoulder-width apart with both of your knees bent and flexible.

Mobility is also important, as we'll discuss later. All footwork and strategic movement should be performed on the balls of your feet. Your weight distribution is also an important factor. Since heavy bag training is dynamic, your weight distribution will frequently change. However, when stationary, keep 50 percent of your body weight on each leg and always be in control of it.

Book One: Heavy Bag Training

Next, the hands are aligned one behind the other along your centerline. The lead arm is held high and bent at approximately 90 degrees. The rear arm is kept back by the chin. Arranged this way, the hands not only protect the upper centerline but also allow quick deployment of your punches as well as other striking techniques.

When holding your guard, do not tighten your shoulder or arm muscles prior to striking. Stay relaxed and loose. Finally, keep your chin slightly angled down. This diminishes target size and reduces the likelihood of a paralyzing blow to your chin or a lethal strike to your throat during an actual self-defense encounter.

If you want to assume a southpaw fighting stance, you would perform the very same steps mentioned above but with your right side facing forward and closest to the bag. Generally, most right handed people with use the orthodox stance, while left handed people will opt for the southpaw.

The Orthodox Fighting Stance.   *The Southpaw Fighting Stance.*

Heavy Bag Bible

However, for those who are interested in reality based self-defense, you must be able to fight your adversary with equal ability on both the right and left sides of your body. This means that you would need to practice heavy bag work from both the southpaw and orthodox stances.

The best method for practicing your fighting stance is in front of a full-length mirror. Place the mirror in an area that allows sufficient room for movement; a garage or basement is perfect. Stand in front of the mirror, far enough away to see your entire body. Stand naturally with your arms relaxed at your sides. Now close your eyes and quickly assume your fighting stance. Open your eyes and check for flaws. Look for low hand guards, improper foot positioning or body angle, rigid shoulders and knees, etc. Drill this way repeatedly, working from both the right and left side. Practice this until your fighting stance becomes second nature.

One common mistake beginners make is to stand squarely in front of the heavy bag without regard to their stance. Never stand squarely in front of the heavy bag. Not only will this expose your centerline targets, it also diminishes your balance, inhibits efficient footwork, and minimizes your reach.

A full-length mirror can also be used for shadow boxing training. Shadow boxing is the creative deployment of offensive and defensive techniques and maneuvers against an imaginary opponent.

Book One: Heavy Bag Training

Pictured here, one of Mr. Franco's students warming up in front of the mirror before his heavy bag workout.

Heavy Bag Bible

Pictured here, the classic "boxer's stance." Notice how the fighter's centerline is angled at approximately 45-degrees.

Avoid the tendency to let both your elbows flair out to the sides. This type of elbow positioning places your hands out of proper body mechanic alignment.

Book One: Heavy Bag Training

Fighting Stance Review

Heavy Bag Bible

You'll Need to Move Around the Bag!

Now that we have the fighting stance covered, it's time to talk about mobility and footwork. One of the biggest mistakes beginners make when working out on the heavy bag, is to just stand in front of it and beat it to death! While this methodology might have some limited street fighting applications, it should not be your sole method of training on the bag. Remember, the heavy bag must swing freely, and this means that you must also be able to move with it.

Footwork & Mobility

I define mobility as the ability to move your body quickly and freely, which is accomplished through basic footwork. The safest footwork involves quick, economical steps performed on the balls of your feet, while you remain relaxed and balanced. Keep in mind that balance is one of the most important considerations when working out on the heavy bag.

Basic footwork can be used for both offensive and defensive purposes, and it is structured around four general directions: forward, backward, right, and left. However, always remember this footwork rule of thumb: *Always move the foot closest to the direction you want to go first, and let the other foot follow an equal distance.* This prevents cross-stepping, which can be disastrous in a high-risk combat situation.

Basic Footwork Movements

1. Moving forward (advance) - from your fighting stance, first move your front foot forward (approximately 12 inches) and then move your rear foot an equal distance.

2. Moving backward (retreat) - from your fighting stance, first move your rear foot backward (approximately 12 inches) and then move your front foot an equal distance.

Book One: Heavy Bag Training

3. Moving right (sidestep right) - from your fighting stance, first move your right foot to the right (approximately 12 inches) and then move your left foot an equal distance.

4. Moving left (sidestep left) - from your fighting stance, first move your left foot to the left (approximately 12 inches) and then move your right foot an equal distance.

Practice these four movements for 10 to 15 minutes a day in front of a full-length mirror. In a couple weeks, your footwork should be quick, balanced, and natural.

Footwork and mobility play a very important role when working out on the heavy bag.

Circling Right and Left

Strategic circling is an advanced form of footwork where you will use your front leg as a pivot point. This type of movement permits you to move 360-degrees around the bag and also allow you to strike from various angles. Strategic circling can be performed from either a left or right stance.

Circling left (from a left stance) - this means you'll be moving your body around the heavy bag in a clockwise direction. From a left stance, step 8 to 12 inches to the left with your left foot, then use your left leg as a pivot point and wheel your entire rear leg to the left until the correct stance and positioning is acquired.

Circling right (from a right stance) - from a right stance, step 8 to 12 inches to the right with your right foot, then use your right leg as a pivot point and wheel your entire rear leg to the right until the correct stance and positioning is acquired.

Reality is the key! Try to visualize the heavy bag as a living breathing opponent who will hit back the moment you let your guard down.

Book One: Heavy Bag Training

Avoid Cross-Stepping When Hitting The Bag

Cross-stepping is the process of crossing one foot in front or behind the other when moving around the bag. Such sloppy footwork makes you vulnerable to a variety of problems. Some include:

- It severely compromises your balance.
- It restricts the offensive flow of punching.
- It limits quick and rapid footwork.
- It can lead to a sprained ankle.

As I said earlier, the best way to avoid cross-stepping is to follow this basic footwork rule of thumb: *Always move the foot closest to the direction you want to go first, and let the other foot follow an equal distance.*

Explosive Footwork

Explosive footwork is another important component of heavy bag training. In fact, this type of dynamic movement plays a vital role in both offensive and defensive fighting. In offense, explosive footwork allows you to rush your target and maintain a devastating compound attack. In defense, it permits you to disengage quickly from the range of an overwhelming assault.

Explosive footwork is predicated on the following five important factors. They include the following:

1. **Basic footwork** - you must first master the basic footwork skills before incorporating ballistic movements.
2. **Proper body posture** - maintaining correct body posture through footwork movements will prevent loss of balance.
3. **Powerful legs** - strong and powerful upper and lower legs will allow you to launch your body effortlessly through the ranges of combat.

57

Heavy Bag Bible

4. **Equal weight distribution** - a noncommittal weight distribution (fifty percent on each leg) will permit you to move instantly in any direction.

5. **Raised heel** - this creates a springlike effect in your footwork movements.

Although there are many components of efficient footwork, moving on the balls of your feet is vital. Flat-footed footwork will slow you down considerably during your bag training.

Book One: Heavy Bag Training

Chapter 4
How to Punch Correctly

Injury Free Punching

Since the majority of your heavy bag techniques will be delivered with your fists, it's essential that you know how to punch without sustaining a hand injury. Essentially, this requires you to understand and ultimately master a few concepts and body mechanic principles. Keep in mind that you do not have to be a professional boxer or martial arts expert to master these fundamental principles.

What Causes Hand Injuries?

There are four main causes of punching related hand injuries. They are incorrect fist configuration, skeletal misalignment, weak hands, wrist and forearms and hitting the wrong anatomical target.

While there are different body mechanics for each and every punch, there are four things that must take place to avoid a hand injury, when hitting the heavy bag. They include the following:

- Knowing how to make a proper fist.
- Possessing strong hands, wrists, and forearms.
- Maintaining skeletal alignment when striking the bag.
- Pinpoint target accuracy.

How to Make a Proper Fist

The first thing you need to do is learn the proper way make a fist. It's ironic that some of the most experienced fighters and martial artists don't know how to make a proper fist. As you can imagine, improper fist clenching can be disastrous for some of the following reasons:

- You can jam, sprain, or break your fingers.
- You can destroy wrist alignment, resulting in a sprained or broken wrist.

Book One: Heavy Bag Training

- **You'll lose significant impact power when hitting the bag.**

To make a proper fist, make sure your fingers are tightly clenched and that your thumb is securely wrapped around your second and third knuckles. Your fist should resemble a solid brick. Remember, if you cannot make a proper fist, you will not be capable of delivering a solid punch on the heavy bag!

Pictured here, the correct way to make a fist.

Long fingernails will compromise the structural integrity of your punch by causing your individual fingers to protrude from your fist. This can easily lead to a severe hand or wrist injury. If you are serious about heavy bag training, consider keeping all of your fingernails very short.

61

You Must Keep Everything Straight

Now that you know how to make a proper fist, your next step is learning how to maintaining skeletal alignment when your fist makes contact with the bag. Skeletal alignment will help ensure that both your hand and wrists will not buckle and break during impact with the heavy bag.

One of the biggest mistakes beginners make when making a fist is allowing their thumbs to protrude outward. This hand position is dangerous and can often lead to hand and finger injuries as well as powerless blows. Remember, always to keep your thumbs tightly wrapped around the other two fingers when throwing punches.

Center Knuckle Contact

In order to maintain skeletal alignment when punching, you need to learn to punch with your center knuckle first. Punching with the center of your knuckle is important because it affords proper alignment and maximizes the impact of your blow.

Excluding hammer fist strikes, every conceivable punch (i.e., jab, rear cross, hook, uppercut, shovel hook, etc) can be delivered with center knuckle contact.

Center knuckle contact also prevents a broken hand or "boxer's fracture" from occurring. Essentially, a boxer's fracture occurs when the small metacarpal bone bends downward and toward the palm of the hand during impact with an extremely hard surface (such as a brick wall or human skull).

Contrary to what karate schools teach, I suggest that you avoid striking the heavy bag with your first two knuckles. This karate style of punching diffuses the weight transfer of the punch which can easily lead to a broken hand.

Wrist and Forearm Alignment

If you want to avoid breaking or spraining your wrists, you must always remember to keep your wrists aligned with your forearm throughout the execution of your punch. This applies to both linear punches (jab, rear cross) as well as circular punches (hooks, uppercuts and shovel hooks).

If your wrist bends or collapses on impact, you will either sprain or break it. It's that simple. Remember, a sprained or broken wrist will set back your bag training for months.

Also, don't make the false assumption that boxing gloves or hands wraps will always keep your wrists straight. I know of several fighters who actually sprained their wrists while wearing both hand wraps and boxing gloves.

If you want to avoid breaking or spraining your wrists, you must always remember to keep your wrists aligned with your forearm throughout the execution of your punch.

Don't make the false assumption that boxing gloves or bag gloves will keep your wrists straight. I can assure you, they won't.

Ironically, one of the best ways to learn how to throw a punch without bending your wrists is to regularly workout on the heavy bag. The heavy bag will provide the necessary amount of resistance to progressively strengthen and condition the bones, tendons and ligaments in your wrists. Just remember to start off slowly and gradually increase the force of your punches.

Strong Hands, Wrists and Forearms

Proper fist configuration and wrist alignment are critical, but that is really only half of the equation. You must have strong hands, wrists, and forearms to withstand the actual force of hitting the heavy bag.

You will, therefore, need to perform specific hand and forearm exercises to strengthen these muscles. Bruce Lee was well aware of this important fact. As a matter of fact, he would religiously strengthen and develop his hands and forearms for the rigors of power punching.

Book One: Heavy Bag Training

Lee knew that powerful and injury free punching depends largely on the overall strength and structural integrity of your hands, wrists and forearms.

Conditioning and Strength Training

There are many efficient ways of strengthening your hands, wrists and forearms for heavy bag training. If you are low on cash and just starting out, you can begin by squeezing a tennis ball a couple times per week. One hundred repetitions per hand would be a good start.

Power Putty

Later on you can add power putty to your hand strengthening routine. This unique hand exerciser is made up of silicone rubber that can be squeezed, pulled, pinched, clawed and stretched in just about any conceivable direction. This tough, resistant putty will strengthen the muscles of your forearm, wrists, hands and fingers.

Hand Grippers

Another quick and effective way to strengthen your hands, wrists and forearms is to work out with heavy duty hand grippers. While there are a wide selection of them on the market, I prefer using the Captains of Crush brand. These high-quality grippers are virtually indestructible and they come in a variety of different resistance levels ranging from 60 to 365 pounds.

Weight Training

Finally, you can condition your wrists and forearms by performing various forearm exercises with free weights. Exercises like hammer curls, reverse curls, wrist curls, and reverse wrist curls are great for developing strong wrists, forearms, and hands. When training your forearms, be sure to work both your extensor and flexor muscles. Here are a few to get you started:

Barbell Wrist Curls

This exercise strengthens the flexor muscles. Perform 5 sets of 8-10 repetitions. To perform the exercise, follow these steps:

1. Sit at the end of a bench, grab a barbell with an underhand grip and place both of your hands close together.
2. In a smooth and controlled fashion, slowly bend your wrists and lower the barbell toward the floor.
3. Contract your forearms and curl the weight back to the starting position.

Reverse Wrist Curls

This exercise develops and strengthens the extensor muscle of the forearm. Perform 6 sets of 6-8 repetitions. To perform the exercise, follow these steps:

1. Sit at the end of a bench, hold a barbell with an overhand grip (your hands should be approximately 11 inches apart) and place your forearms on top of your thighs.
2. Slowly lower the barbell as far as your wrists will allow.
3. Flex your wrists upward back to the starting position.

Behind-the-Back Wrist Curls

This exercise strengthens both the flexor muscles of the forearms. Perform 5 sets of 6-8 repetitions To perform the exercise, follow these steps:

1. Hold a barbell behind your back at arm's length (your hands should be approximately shoulder-width apart).
2. Uncurl your finger and let the barbell slowly roll down your palms.
3. Close your hands and roll the barbell back into your hands.

Hammer Curls

This exercise strengthens both the Brachialis and Brachioradialis muscles. Perform 5 sets of 8-10 repetitions. To perform the exercise, follow these steps:

1. Stand with both feet approximately shoulder-width apart, with both dumbbells at your sides.
2. Keeping your elbows close to your body and your palms facing inward, slowly curl both dumbbells upward towards your shoulders.

3. Slowly return to the starting position.

Reverse Barbell Curls

Reverse curls can be a great alternative to hammer curls. This exercise strengthens both the Brachialis and Brachioradialis muscles. Perform 5 sets of 8-10 repetitions. To perform the exercise, follow these steps:

1. Stand with both feet approximately shoulder width apart. Hold a barbell with your palms facing down (pronated grip).
2. Keeping your upper arms stationary, curl the weights up until the bar is at shoulder level.
3. Slowly return to the starting position.

Accuracy Counts!

The final component of injury free punching is target accuracy. For example, in a real world self-defense encounter you must avoid hitting hard body surfaces like the opponent's skull.

Believe it or not, many self-defense hand injuries are a result of striking the opponent's skull, which is extremely hard and resilient. It is likened to a crash helmet that protects the human brain from all forms of impact. I know several fighters who broke their hands when their fists connected with an opponent's forehead or skull.

Similarly, in heavy bag training, you too must be careful where you place your punches. It's important that your strikes are accurate, and your punches are timed correctly. This can be especially challenging considering that the heavy bag is always moving in unpredictable directions. Just keep in mind that one misplaced power punch can easily sprain or break your wrist.

Book One: Heavy Bag Training

Since the heavy bag is constantly moving, you need to be especially careful timing the delivery of your punches.

Be Aware of What You Are Doing!

Learning how to punch correctly also means you will have to study and observe each and every punch in your arsenal and make certain they can handle the rigors of heavy bag work. Through proper analytical observation, you can quickly identify the strengths and weaknesses of each punch in your arsenal. The best way to accomplish this is to methodically test each punch on the heavy bag.

For example, take the most basic punch known to man - the rear cross. For those who may not be aware, the rear cross is one of the most powerful punches in a fighter's arsenal.

Heavy Bag Bible

Begin by standing approximately four to five feet from the bag. Then, assume a fighting stance with your left leg forward and your body positioned at a forty-five degree angle from the bag. Make certain both of your hands are properly clenched into fists and your head and chin are angled slightly down.

Now, deliver the punch, exhale and quickly twist and throw your rear arm and shoulder forward and towards the heavy bag. Make certain to twist your rear leg, hip and shoulder forward and extend your rear arm straight. Do not lock out your rear arm when throwing the punch, be certain there is a slight bend in the elbow. Your punch should forcefully snap into the bag and then return to the starting position. For more information about the rear cross, see Chapter 5.

After delivering the punch to the heavy bag, make the following important observations:

- What was the overall feeling of the punch when you delivered it? Did it feel rigid and forced or was it loose and fluid?
- What happened when your punch connected with the bag? Did the punch snap or crack the heavy bag? Or did it just nudge it?
- Did anything feel strained or hurt when your fist initially connected with the bag?
- Was your punch accurate? Did you hit the bag exactly where you intended?
- Did you remember to exhale or did you hold your breath when you threw the punch?
- What happened to the structural integrity of your fist when you make contact with the punching bag? Did your fists open? Did your thumb get in the way? Did your wrist buckle inward?
- Which knuckle made initial contact with the punching bag?

You also might want to consider video taping yourself so you can quickly identify mistakes and errors in your punching form. Or perhaps you can have your training partner observe your punching technique and give you constructive feedback.

The Punching Mitts

If you find the heavy bag to be a bit intimidating to work with, you can always start off with the punching mitts (also called focus mitts) to examine your punching form.

Unlike the heavy bag, the punching mitts are more forgiving on your wrists and hands and will allow you to gradually build up your power as your punching form improves.

Punching mitts will challenge even the most seasoned fighter by improving both offensive and defensive fighting skills, punching speed, stamina, rhythm, endurance, accuracy, timing, reflexes, footwork, punching combinations, punching power and counter punching techniques.

The only downside to working with the punching mitts is they will require a training partner to hold them for you. The good news is, once you have trained on the mitts, you can then finally graduate to the heavy bag.

Heavy Bag Bible

Book One: Heavy Bag Training

Chapter 5
Heavy Bag Techniques

Fighting Ranges

Before we get into specific heavy bag techniques, you first need to understand that the distance and angle of the heavy bag will often dictate which striking technique you can execute at any given moment. Therefore, you must know about the three fighting ranges. They include: kicking, punching, and grappling range.

Kicking Range

The furthest distance is kicking range. At this range you are usually too far away to punch the heavy bag, so you would use your legs to make contact. Kicking range techniques are powerful and can give your legs a tremendous workout.

Important: If you are strictly interested in heavy bag training for boxing, you can skip this section and focus exclusively on Section 2 of this chapter.

While there are a myriad of kicking techniques in the martial arts world, here's a list of some of the basic kicking techniques you can use on the heavy bag:

- Push kick (front leg)
- Push kick (back leg)
- Side kick (front leg)
- Hook kick (front leg)
- Hook kick (back leg)

If you are going to execute kicking techniques in a real fight, always employ low-line kicks to targets below the assailant's waist. They are efficient, effective, deceptive, non-telegraphic, and relatively safe. Low-line targets include the groin, quadriceps, common peroneal nerve (approximately 4 inches above the knee area), knee, and shin.

Book One: Heavy Bag Training

Pictured here, the kicking range.

Push Kick (from the front leg)

1. To perform the kick, begin from an orthodox stance (left side forward).
2. While maintaining your balance, shift your weight onto your back leg and raise your front leg up (your front knee should be bent at approximately 90 degrees).
3. Next, thrust with your hips and drive the ball of your front foot into the heavy bag.
4. After contact is made with the bag, quickly retract your leg to the starting position. Remember to always keep your hands up when performing kicking techniques.

Heavy Bag Bible

When performing the push kick on the heavy bag, be certain to make contact with the ball of your foot and not your toes. Striking the bag with your toes can easily lead to a severe injury.

Here, the fighter delivers a push kick from his front leg.

Push Kick (from the rear leg)

1. To perform the kick, begin from an orthodox stance (left side forward).

2. While maintaining your balance, push your back foot off the ground and shift your weight to your front leg (your rear knee should be bent at approximately 90 degrees).

3. Next, thrust with your hips and drive the ball of your foot into

the heavy bag.

4. After contact is made with the bag, quickly retract your leg to the starting position. Again, make certain to make contact with the ball of your foot and not your toes.

Side Kick (from the front leg)

1. The side kick is a powerful linear kick executed from the lead leg. Contact is made with the heel of your foot. To perform the kick, begin from an orthodox stance (left side facing the heavy bag).
2. While maintaining your balance, lean back and shift your weight onto your rear leg while simultaneously pivoting your body so your centerline is approximately 90 degrees from the bag.
3. Raise your front knee up and close to your body (this is called the "chamber" position).
4. Next, use your hips and thrust your front leg forcefully into the bag. Contact is made with the heel of your foot.
5. After contact is made with the heavy bag, retract your leg to the starting position.

Here are two common mistakes that occur when executing a side kick: (1) Failure to chamber your leg - your kick will have no force. To remedy this, lift your leg to the bent-knee position (this is known as a moderate chamber position). (2) Your toes lead the extension - you will jam your toes and sprain your ankle. To remedy this, pull your toes back toward your knee. This will ensure that your kick is leading with the heel of your foot.

Heavy Bag Bible

While kicking above the waist is not recommended for street combat, you can still add them to your heavy bag workouts.

One of the most important considerations when executing a side kick is maintaining proper skeletal alignment. Skeletal alignment is the proper alignment or arrangement of your body, which maximizes the structural integrity of your striking limb. Therefore, when executing a side kick, always make certain that the heel, knee, and hip of your kicking leg are properly aligned.

Hook kick (front leg)

1. To perform the hook kick from your front leg, begin from an orthodox stance (left side facing the heavy bag).
2. While maintaining your balance, lean back slightly and shift your weight to your rear leg.
3. Simultaneously raise your front knee up and towards the bag.
4. Next, quickly twist your front hip and swing your lead leg forcefully into the bag. Your front knee should be slightly bent when impact is made with the target. Avoid snapping your knee when performing the kick. Contact should be made with either the dorsum of your foot or shin bone.
5. After contact is made with the heavy bag, bring your leg back to the starting position.

In this photo, the fighter performs a hook kick with his front leg.

Hook kick (rear leg)

1. To perform the hook kick from your rear leg, begin from an orthodox stance (left side facing the heavy bag).
2. While maintaining your balance, push off the back foot and shift your weight forward.
3. Next, raise your rear knee up and twist your hips forward as you swing your rear leg forcefully into the bag.
4. Your rear knee should be slightly bent when impact is made with the bag. Avoid snapping your knee when performing the hook kick. Once again, contact should be made with either the dorsum of your foot or shin bone.
5. After contact is made with the bag, bring your leg back to the starting position.

The hook kick is also a devastating self-defense technique that can collapse and temporarily immobilize the assailant's leg. Keep in mind that if you strike the assailant's knee you can cause permanent damage to the cartilage, ligaments, tendons and bones.

Book One: Heavy Bag Training

While the traditional round house kick might look similar to the hook kick, it differs significantly. Round house kicks are generally snapping kicks generated from the knee, while hook kicks are driving kicks that generate tremendous power from the hips. Pictured here, a woman performs a traditional round house kick on the heavy bag.

Heavy Bag Bible

Heavy bag training is not limited to any particular style of fighting. Here, a traditional martial artist performs a groin kick on the bag.

When performing kicking technique on the heavy bag, try to avoid remaining stationary. Get into the habit of constantly moving around the heavy bag with quick and economical steps.

Punching Range

The next distance of fighting is punching range and it's the mid-range of combat. At this distance, you are close enough to the bag to strike it with your fists. Punching range techniques should be quick and efficient and they should be the foundation of your heavy bag arsenal.

For those of you who are interested in reality based self-defense training, I strongly encourage you to specialize in the punching range. Here are just a few reasons why:

- The opponent's defensive reaction time is reduced in punching range.
- Unlike kicking techniques, you can efficiently neutralize your adversary with punches and other hand strikes.
- Compared to the other ranges of unarmed combat, punching range techniques are more efficient - there is less energy expenditure.
- Punching range techniques are less telegraphic than kicking range tools.
- Compared to grappling range (vertical & horizontal planes), punching range only requires moderate bodily commitment.
- Unlike kicking range, there is less "space requirement" necessary to deploy most of your punching range techniques.
- Unlike grappling range combat, there is virtually no bodily entanglement, so multiple assailants can be fought in the punching range of unarmed combat.

Heavy Bag Bible

Punching Techniques and Western Boxing

Punching range is the midrange of unarmed fighting. At this distance, you are close enough to the heavy bag to strike with your hands fists. Interestingly enough, amateur and professional boxers focus exclusively on this range of unarmed combat.

Here's a list of some of the punching techniques that you can perform on the heavy bag.

- Jab
- Rear cross (also called the straight right)
- Hook punch
- Uppercut punch

The punching range.

Book One: Heavy Bag Training

Very little has changed since the golden age of boxing. Amateur and professional boxers alike focus exclusively on punching techniques for their sport.

Heavy Bag Bible

The Jab

The jab is a foundation technique for boxers and mixed martial artists. This punch is thrown from your front hand and it has a quick snap when delivered.

1. Start off in a fighting stance with both of your hands held up in the guard position. Your fists should be lightly clenched with both of your elbows pointing to the ground.
2. To perform the punch, simultaneously step toward the bag and twist your front waist and shoulder forward as you snap your front arm into the bag.
3. When delivering the punch, remember not to lock out your arm as this will have a "pushing effect" on the heavy bag.
4. Quickly retract your arm back to the starting position.

One common mistake when throwing the jab is to let it deflect off to the side of the bag. Also, keep in mind that jabs can be delivered to the head (top of the heavy bag) or the body (middle of the bag).

When executing linear punches (i.e. jabs, rear crosses, etc) on the heavy bag, remember that your line of initiation should always be your line of retraction. Avoid arcing or dropping your blow after contact is made with the bag. Such sloppy body mechanics will throw you off balance and diminish your impact power.

Book One: Heavy Bag Training

In boxing and mixed martial arts, the jab is an essential punch used to throw the opponent off balance, set him up for other blows, test his reflexes, and keep him from moving toward you.

Using the Jab for Street Self-Defense

While the jab might be appropriate for boxing, mixed martial arts and other forms of combat sport competition, it has no purpose in real world combat. The truth is the jab is combatively deficient for some of the following reasons:

- It lacks neutralizing power.
- It can expose you to a counter attack.
- It often agitates the assailant more than it harms him.
- It prolongs a self defense altercation and allows the assailant the opportunity to escalate his level of force against you.
- It's a probing and point scoring tool.

If self-defense is your interest and concern, you can simply replace the Jab with the Lead Straight punch. Like the jab, the lead straight is also a linear punch thrown from your lead arm, however this punch is much more powerful and can be used on the heavy bag as well as real life self-defense situations.

Book One: Heavy Bag Training

The lead straight is a linear punch thrown from your lead arm and contact is made with the center knuckle. To execute the lead straight, quickly twist your lead leg, hip, and shoulder forward. Snap your blow into the assailant's target and return back to the starting position. A common mistake is to throw the punch and let it deflect off to the side of the heavy bag.

Rear Cross

The rear cross (also called the straight right) is considered the heavy artillery of punches and it's thrown from your rear arm. To execute the punch, perform the following steps:

1. Start off in a fighting stance with both of your hands held up in the guard position. Your fists should be lightly clenched with both of your elbows pointing to the ground.

2. To perform the punch, quickly twist your rear hips and shoulders forward as you snap your rear arm into the heavy bag. Proper waist twisting and weight transfer is of paramount importance to the rear cross. You must shift your weight from your rear foot to your lead leg as you throw the punch.

3. To maximize the impact of the punch, make certain that your fist is positioned horizontally. Avoid overextending the blow or exposing your chin during its execution.

4. Once again, do not lock out your arm when throwing the punch. Let the power of the punch sink into the bag before you retract it back to the starting position.

Heavy Bag Bible

The rear cross is an extremely powerful punch that can be delivered to both high and low targets on the heavy bag.

Book One: Heavy Bag Training

When throwing the rear cross, be certain not to lock your elbow. Elbow locking is a common problem among novices. There should always be a slight bend in your elbow when the punch hits the bag. Remember, if your elbow locks upon impact, it will have a "pushing effect" and rob you of critical knock-out power.

Another common mistake when throwing the rear cross on the bag is to let the punch glide downwards after contact is made. Always remember, the trajectory of initiating your punch must also be the very same trajectory of retracting your punch.

When delivering the rear cross, remember to turn your palm down so your fists hit the bag horizontally.

Remember to completely tighten your fists when impact is made with the heavy bag. This action will allow your natural body weapon to travel with optimum speed and efficiency, and it will also augment the impact power of your punch.

Hook Punch

The hook is another devastating punch in your arsenal of techniques, yet it's also one of the most difficult to master. This punch can be performed from either your front or rear hand and it can be thrown high or low to the heavy bag. There are actually two variations of the hook punch, they include:

- **Traditional Hook Punch**
- **Modified Hook Punch**

For the purposes of this book, I will teach you the traditional hook punch that is used in most boxing circles. Once again, if you would like to learn about the modified hook punch, which is used exclusively for street self-defense applications, you might want to look into my other books for more information.

1. Start in a fighting stance with your hand guard held up.
2. To execute the hook punch, quickly and smoothly, raise your elbow up so that your arm is parallel to the ground while simultaneously torquing your shoulder, hip, and foot into the

Book One: Heavy Bag Training

direction of the blow.

3. When delivering the strike, be certain your arm is bent at least ninety degrees and that your wrist and forearm are kept straight throughout the movement.

4. As you throw the punch, your fist is positioned horizontally. The elbow should be locked when contact is made with the heavy bag.

5. Return back to the starting position.

When delivering the hook punch, remember to maintain the proper wrist, forearm and shoulder alignment at all times.

The hook is one of the most devastating blows in your arsenal. However, it's also one of the most difficult to master. To properly execute the hook punch, you must maintain the proper wrist, forearm, and shoulder alignment. When delivering the strike, be certain your arm is bent at least ninety degrees and that your wrist and forearm are kept straight throughout the entire movement.

93

Heavy Bag Bible

The modified hook punch is specifically suited for reality based self-defense applications. In this photo, notice how the practitioner's fist is positioned vertically.

Uppercut Punch

The uppercut is a another powerful punch that can be delivered from both the lead and rear arm. Due to its unusual angle of delivery, the uppercut is best practiced on either the punching mitts or uppercut bag. However, with a bit of careful practice it can be practiced on the heavy bag.

1. Start off in a fighting stance with both of your hands held up in the guard position. Your fists should be lightly clenched with both of your elbows pointing to the ground.
2. To execute the uppercut, drop your shoulder and bend your knees.
3. Quickly, stand up and drive your fist upward and into the heavy bag. Your palm should be facing you when contact is made with the heavy bag. To avoid any possible injury, keep your wrists straight.
4. Make certain that the punch has a tight arc and that you avoid any and all "winding up" motions. A properly executed uppercut should be a tight punch and should feel like an explosive jolt.
5. Return back to the fighting stance.

The real key to delivering a powerful uppercut punch is the lifting of your legs into the direction of your blow.

Heavy Bag Bible

Pictured here, the rear uppercut punch.

In the early 1800's, the famous boxer pioneer, Samuel Elias (also known as Dutch Sam), was responsible for discovering the right hand "undercut" which was later called the uppercut.

Book One: Heavy Bag Training

There are two major problems with the uppercut featured in this photo. First, the practitioner is too far from the heavy bag. Second, he's curling his wrists which can easily lead to a sprain or break.

When performing the uppercut, avoid any and all wind up motions. This is what you should not do!

Heavy Bag Bible

While the uppercut punch is best suited for the punching mitts, it can also be practiced on the heavy bag. Just remember to keep your wrists straight when making contact with the bag.

Grappling Range

The third and closest range of fighting is grappling range. At this distance, you are too close to the bag to kick or execute linear punches, so you would use close-quarter strikes.

Grappling range is actually divided into two different planes; vertical and horizontal. In the vertical plane, you would deliver impact techniques, some of which include elbow and knee strikes, head butts, gouging and crushing tactics, and biting and tearing techniques.

In the horizontal plane of grappling range, you are ground fighting with your opponent and can deliver all of the previously mentioned techniques, including various submission holds, locks and chokes.

When it comes to heavy bag training, grappling range striking techniques are going to appeal to three groups of people:

- **Self-defense practitioners**
- **Mixed martial artists (MMA)**
- **Martial artists (traditional and eclectics)**

You can add a couple grappling range strikes to your heavy bag workouts. Here are two:

- **Elbow strikes**
- **Knee strikes**

Combining offensive strikes from all three ranges of fighting (kicking, punching and grappling) during your heavy bag workouts will thoroughly condition your body from head to toe.

Heavy Bag Bible

The Grappling range.

Horizontal Elbow

The elbows are devastating weapons that can be used in the grappling range. They are explosive, deceptive and very difficult to stop. Elbows can generally be delivered horizontally, vertically, diagonally and they can be thrown from either your front or rear arm.

Let's just take a look at the body mechanics of the horizontal elbow strike

1. Start off in a fighting stance with both of your hands held up in the guard position. Make certain that you are standing in close proximity to the heavy bag.
2. To execute the elbow strike, quickly and smoothly, raise your elbow up so that your arm is parallel to the ground.
3. Next, simultaneously torquing your shoulder, hip, and foot

Book One: Heavy Bag Training

into the direction of the bag. The tip of your elbow should make contact with the target.

4. Return back to the starting position.

Pictured here, a horizontal elbow strike delivered from the rear arm.

Be careful when delivering elbow strikes on a canvas heavy bag. The material can quickly tear up the skin on your elbows, leaving your bag permanently strained with blood.

Diagonal Knee Strike

The knee strike is another devastating close-quarter grappling range tool that can do a lot of damage. The knee strike can also be delivered diagonally or vertically to the heavy bag.

Here are the body mechanics of the diagonal knee strike.

1. To perform the diagonal knee strike from your rear leg, begin from an orthodox stance (left side facing the heavy bag).
2. Next, grab hold of the bag with both hands.
3. While maintaining your balance, push off the back foot and shift your weight forward.
4. Next, raise your rear knee up and swing your hips and rear leg diagonally into the bag.
5. Your rear knee should be sharply bent when impact is made with the bag.
6. After contact is made, bring your leg back to the starting position.

When delivering knee strikes, keep your rear leg bent with your toe pointed to the ground. This toe position helps maintain proper skeletal alignment; protects your toes from unnecessary injury; and facilitates quick and rapid delivery.

Book One: Heavy Bag Training

The diagonal knee strike.

Vertical Knee Strike

1. To perform the vertical knee strike from your rear leg, begin from an orthodox stance (left side facing the heavy bag).
2. Next, grab hold of the bag with both hands.
3. While maintaining your balance, push off the back foot and shift your weight forward.
4. Next, raise your rear knee up and drive your hips and rear leg vertically into the heavy bag.
5. Your rear knee should be sharply bent when impact is made with the bag.
6. After contact is made with the bag, bring your leg back to the starting position.

Book One: Heavy Bag Training

Chapter 6
Heavy Bag Workouts

Three Heavy Bag Training Methods

Over the past thirty years of teaching the martial arts, I have developed three unique training methodologies that can be applied to heavy bag training. They include Proficiency, Conditioning and Street Training. Let's take a look at each one.

Conditioning Training

Conditioning Training is primarily used by boxers, mixed martial artists, kickboxers, self-defense technicians and fitness enthusiasts who wish to train on the heavy bag for specified period of time called "rounds". Depending on the practitioner's level of conditioning, each round can range anywhere from one to five minutes. Each round is then separated by either 30-second, one-minute or two-minute breaks. A good heavy bag workout consists of at least five to eight rounds.

Conditioning Training is performed at a moderate pace, and it develops cardiovascular fitness, muscular endurance, fluidity, rhythm, distancing, timing, speed, footwork, and balance. Many fitness enthusiasts looking to burn fat will use this methodology as it tends to burn a significant amount of calories.

Conditioning Training does require that you have a fundamental understanding of piecing punches and kicks together into logical combinations.

Proficiency Training

The second training methodology is Proficiency Training and it's generally used by martial artists and self-defense practitioners who want to sharpen one specific punch, kick, or strike at a time by executing it over and over for a prescribed number of repetitions. Each time the technique is performed with "clean" form at various speeds. Punches are also performed with the eyes closed to develop a kinesthetic "feel" for the action.

Proficiency Training on the heavy bag develops speed, power, accuracy, non-telegraphic movement, balance, and general psychomotor skill.

Street Training

The third and final training methodology is Street Training, and it's specially designed for reality-based self-defense preparation.

Since most self-defense altercations are explosive, lasting an average of 20 seconds, the practitioner must prepare for this possible scenario. This means delivering explosive and powerful compound attacks with vicious intent for approximately 20 seconds, resting one minute, and then repeating the process.

Street Training prepares you for the stress and immediate fatigue of a real fight. It also develops speed, power, explosiveness, target selection and recognition, timing, footwork and breath control.

Designing Your Heavy Bag Workout

While all three training methodologies are important, we are going to focus exclusively on Conditioning Training, which means we are going to focus on "time based" workouts.

Time Based Workouts

Essentially, a time based heavy bag workout is based on "rounds" and it's an ideal way to structure your workouts. Before you begin, now is the time to decide on the duration of your rounds as well as the rest intervals.

In most cases, mixed martial artists, boxers and kick boxers will

Heavy Bag Bible

work the heavy bag for three-minute rounds with one-minute rest periods. Depending on their level of conditioning and specific training goals, they might do this for a total of 5 to 8 rounds.

Initially, you'll need to experiment with both the round duration and rest intervals to see what works best for you. Remember to start off slow and progressively build up the intensity and duration of your workouts. Remember to work with the bag and not try to kill it!

To get you started, here are some sample time-based workouts you might want to try. Keep in mind, the Advanced Level workouts are for elite fighters who have a minimum of 5 years of heavy bag training and

Sample Time Based Heavy Bag Workouts

Skill Level	Duration of Each Round	Rest Period	Total Number of rounds
Beginner	1 minute	2 minutes	3
Beginner	1 minute	1 minute	3
Beginner	2 minutes	2 minute	3
Beginner	2 minutes	1 minute	3
Intermediate	3 minutes	2 minutes	5
Intermediate	3 minutes	1 minute	5
Intermediate	3 minutes	2 minute	6
Intermediate	3 minutes	1 minute	6
Advanced	4 minutes	2 minutes	8
Advanced	4 minutes	1 minute	8
Advanced	5 minutes	2 minutes	10
Advanced	5 minutes	1 minute	10

conditioning.

A Word of Caution!

Take your time when working out on the bag. If you are learning how to use the heavy bag for the very first time, I strongly urge you to take your time and develop the proper punching and kicking body mechanics before tearing into the bag.

Remember, the heavy bag is a serious piece of training equipment, and it is easy to get injured when using it. Heavy bag workouts are also tough and very demanding. Avoid premature exhaustion by pacing yourself during your workouts. Remember, it's not a race! Enjoy the process of learning how to use the bag with skill and finesse.

Warning! Before you begin any exercise program, including those suggested in this book, it is important to check with your doctor to see if you have any condition that might be aggravated by strenuous exercise.

What is a Combination?

A combination or "compound attack" is the logical sequence of two or more techniques thrown in strategic succession. For example, a jab followed immediately by a rear cross is considered to be a punching combination.

There are an infinite amount of fighting combinations you can perform on the heavy bag. Frankly, you are only limited by your own imagination.

When reading the combination sequence, please note that the word "high" indicates punches delivered at head level on the heavy bag and the word "low" indicates punches delivered at the stomach level on the bag.

Punching Combinations

What follows are just a few punching combinations you can employ in your heavy bag workouts. If you require advanced heavy bag combination training, including step-by-step photographs, please see my book, *Heavy Bag Combinations: The Ultimate Guide to Heavy Bag Punching Combinations.*

- Jab (high) - Jab (high)
- Jab (low) - Jab (low)
- Jab (high) - Jab (low)
- Jab (low) - Jab (high)
- Jab (high) - Jab (high) - Rear Cross (high)
- Jab (high) - Jab (high) - Rear Cross (low)
- Jab - Rear Cross (high)
- Jab - Rear Cross (low)
- Jab - Rear Cross (high) - Jab
- Jab - Rear Cross (low) - Jab
- Jab - Rear Cross - Jab - Rear Cross
- Jab - Jab - Rear Cross
- Jab - Rear Cross - Jab
- Jab - Rear Cross - Lead Hook (high)
- Jab - Rear Cross - Lead Hook (low)
- Jab - Rear Cross - Lead Hook (high) - Rear Hook (high)
- Jab - Rear Cross - Lead Hook (low) - Rear Hook (low)
- Jab - Rear Cross - Lead Hook (high) - Rear Hook (low)

Book One: Heavy Bag Training

Heavy Bag Bible

- Jab - Rear Cross - Lead Hook (low) - Rear Hook (high)
- Jab - Rear Hook (high)
- Jab - Rear Hook (low)
- Jab - Lead Hook (high)
- Jab - Lead Hook (low)
- Jab - Lead Hook (high) - Rear hook (high)
- Jab - Lead Hook (low) - Rear hook (low)
- Jab - Lead Hook (high) - Rear hook (low)
- Jab - Lead Hook (low) - Rear hook (high)
- Jab - Jab - Rear Cross - Lead Hook (high)
- Jab - Jab - Rear Cross - Lead Hook (low)
- Jab - Rear Cross - Lead Hook (high) - Rear Uppercut
- Jab - Rear Cross - Lead Hook (high) - Rear Hook (low) - Lead Uppercut
- Rear Cross - Horizontal Elbow (front)
- Rear Cross - Horizontal Elbow (front) - Horizontal Elbow (rear)
- Rear Cross - Horizontal Elbow (front) - Horizontal Elbow (rear) -Diagonal Knee (front)
- Rear Uppercut - Lead Hook (high)
- Rear Uppercut - Lead Hook (low)
- Rear Uppercut - Lead Hook (high) - Rear Hook (high)
- Rear Uppercut - Lead Hook (low) - Rear Hook (low)
- Rear Uppercut - Lead Hook (high) - Rear Hook (low)

Book One: Heavy Bag Training

Always keep your hands up when throwing combinations on the heavy bag. Notice how the practitioner in this photo delivers a solid jab while keeping his rear hand up.

Heavy Bag Bible

Kicking and Punching Combinations

Here are some kicking and punching combinations you can add to your heavy bag workouts:

- Jab - Hook Kick (rear leg)
- Jab - Jab - Hook Kick (rear leg)
- Jab - Rear Cross - Hook Kick (front leg)
- Jab - Rear Cross - Hook Kick (front leg) - Hook Kick (rear)
- Jab - Diagonal Knee (rear)
- Jab - Diagonal Knee (rear) - Diagonal Knee (front)
- Jab - Diagonal Knee (rear) - Horizontal elbow (front)
- Jab - Rear Cross - Diagonal Knee (front)
- Jab - Rear Cross - Push Kick (rear)
- Jab - Rear Cross - Jab - Rear Cross - Hook Kick (rear)
- Jab - Rear Cross - Jab - Rear Cross - Push Kick (rear)
- Jab - Rear Cross - Push Kick (rear) - Diagonal Knee (front)
- Jab - Rear Cross - Push Kick (rear) - Hook Kick (front)
- Jab - Rear Cross - Diagonal Knee (front) - Horizontal Elbow (rear)
- Push Kick (front leg) - Rear Cross (high)
- Push Kick (front leg) - Rear Cross (low)
- Push Kick (front leg) - Rear Cross (high) - Lead Hook (high)
- Push Kick (front leg) - Rear Cross (low) - Lead Hook (low)
- Push Kick (front leg) - Rear Cross (low) - Lead Hook (high)
- Push Kick (front leg) - Rear Cross (high) - Lead Hook (low)
- Push Kick (front leg) - Rear Cross (high) - Lead Hook (high) - Rear Hook (high)

Book One: Heavy Bag Training

Since most women have small hands and wrists, they need to be especially careful when punching the bag. Proper hand protection is vital!

Heavy Bag Bible

- Push Kick (front leg) - Rear Cross (high) - Lead Hook (low) - Rear Hook (low)
- Push Kick (front leg) - Rear Uppercut
- Push Kick (front leg) - Rear Uppercut - Lead Uppercut
- Push Kick (front leg) - Rear Uppercut - Lead Uppercut - Diagonal Knee (rear)
- Hook Kick (front) - Rear Cross (high)
- Hook Kick (front) - Rear Cross (low)
- Hook Kick (front) - Rear Cross (high) - Lead Hook (high)
- Hook Kick (front) - Rear Cross (high) - Lead Hook (low)
- Hook Kick (front) - Rear Hook (high) - Rear Hook (high)
- Hook Kick (front) - Rear Hook (low) - Rear Hook (low)
- Hook Kick (front) - Rear Hook (high) - Rear Hook (low)
- Hook Kick (front) - Rear Hook (low) - Rear Hook (high)
- Side Kick (front) - Jab - Rear Cross
- Side Kick (front) - Jab - Rear Cross - Lead Hook
- Side Kick (front) - Rear Cross
- Side Kick (front) - Rear Cross - Lead Straight
- Side Kick (front) - Rear Cross - Horizontal Elbow (front)
- Side Kick (front) - Rear Cross - Horizontal Elbow (front) - Horizontal Elbow (rear)
- Side Kick (front) - Rear Cross - Hook Kick (front)
- Side Kick (front) - Diagonal Knee (rear)
- Side Kick (front) - Diagonal Knee (rear) - Horizontal Elbow (front)

Book One: Heavy Bag Training

Avoid hitting canvas heavy bags bare handed. They will lacerate your fingers and knuckles and permanently stain your heavy bag with blood.

Create Your Own Combinations

Use this section to write down your own heavy bag combinations.

1.
2.
3.
4.
5.
6.
7.
8.
9.
10.
11.
12.
13.
14.
15.
16.
17.
18.
19.

Book One: Heavy Bag Training

20.

21.

22.

23.

24.

25.

26.

27.

28.

29.

30.

31.

32.

33.

34.

35.

36.

37.

38.

39.

40.

More Heavy Bag Workout Tips

- Before you begin a heavy bag program, make certain that you have been cleared by your doctor. Since there is always some risk involved in training and because each person is unique, it is important that before beginning any type of training program, you should have a complete physical examination by your physician.
- Before hitting the heavy bag, always warm up with some light stretching and calisthenics.
- Always start your first round on the heavy bag with light punches and kicks. Never go all out in the beginning of your workout session.
- When hitting the bag, never sacrifice proper technique for power or speed.
- Always throw your punching or kicking techniques from a good fighting stance.
- Don't chew gum when working out on the bag.
- Avoid wearing watches and jewelry when training.
- Consider shadow boxing with light dumbbells to strengthen your arm and shoulders for heavy bag work.
- Never hold your breath. Remember to exhale with the delivery of each and every technique.
- Before you invest your time and money in a heavy bag program, it's important to first define your goals. What do you hope to accomplish by training on the bag? For example, do you want to get in better shape? Build up your confidence? Handle a vicious street thug? Enter a mixed martial arts competition?

Book One: Heavy Bag Training

If you have a training partner, he can lend some assistance by holding the heavy bag while you strike it. This can be particularly helpful because your partner can give you "real time" feedback while you are training.

Heavy Bag Bible

- Be cognizant of your distance from the bag at all times. Stand too close when punching the bag will result in a "pushing effect" while standing too far will just cause the blow to simply glance the target.
- When working out alone, avoid the urge to stop the bag from moving. Let it swing freely!
- Avoid the habit of tapping your gloves together before delivering a punch on the bag.
- If you don't know the proper way to throw a punch or kick, get instruction from a qualified coach or instructor.
- Avoid locking out your elbows when punching the bag.
- Be mobile when working out on the bag, avoid stationary punching.

Avoid pulling your free hand back when throwing a punch. Instead, keep your free hand tight and close to your face when punching. In this photo, the practitioner demonstrates a common mistake beginners make when hitting the heavy bag.

Book One: Heavy Bag Training

Heavy Bag Bible

- Avoid premature exhaustion by pacing yourself during your heavy bag workouts.
- Heavy bags don't hit back, so be aware of your own target openings and vulnerabilities when hitting the bag.
- Never let children play or swing from a heavy bag.
- Remember to maintain your balance at all times when punching the bag - never sacrifice your balance for power.

Bare knuckle training should only be performed by experienced practitioners.

- Heavy bags are unforgiving on your body and will certainly test the structural integrity of you punches and blows. Please remember to keep your wrists straight when your fists hit the bag. Learn to gradually build up the force of your blows - a beginner's wrists are usually too weak to accommodate full force strikes on the punching bag.
- When using the heavy bag learn to relax and avoid unnecessarily tensing your arm and shoulder muscles.

Book One: Heavy Bag Training

Muscular tension will throw off the timing of your punches, retard the speed of your blows, kicks and strikes and most certainly wear you out during your heavy bag workout.

- Heavy bags often cause fighters to "lose their form" when delivering their blows. Try to be constantly aware of your form when hitting the bag or better yet have a training partner, teacher or coach observe you when working out on the bag. Another suggestion is to video tape yourself using the punching bag. This will give you a good idea of what you are doing in your workouts.
- Avoid heavy bag training two days in a row. Give your body a few days to recover from your last workout.

When working out alone, avoid the tendency to stop the heavy bag from swinging. Remember, one of the advantages of heavy bag training is to learn to throw combinations at a moving target.

Heavy Bag Bible

- To avoid injury or "burn out", don't engage in heavy bag training more than three times per week.

- Get into the habit of regularly inspecting your heavy bag for tears and other signs of wear.

- Avoid the latest gimmicks - Every so often, some cleaver marketing company will come up with a trendy gimmick that can be added to your heavy bag workouts. Keep your workouts pure and simple. Beginners should avoid adding hand weights, weighted bag gloves, resistance bands and elevations masks to their workouts.

- While most people use the heavy bag for boxing, kickboxing and mixed martial arts training, don't forget the punching bag is a fantastic tool for developing effective self-defense techniques.

- Remember that heavy bag training for combat sports is much different than heavy bag training for real world self-defense scenarios.

- Unless you are highly skilled martial artist, do not kick a heavy bag while bare foot.

- Stay hydrated when working out on the bag. Dehydration can have a real negative effect on your workout, and it can also be dangerous. When working out, always drink plenty of water. Always hydrate before your workout by drinking at least one pint of water. During the summer months, drink more water than usual. Also get into the habit of taking a water bottle with you to your workouts.

- When purchasing heavy bag gear, spare no expense. Heavy bag training is a serious matter, and your training gear should reflect it. Good equipment will provide years of reliable use and enhance your fighting skills.

Book One: Heavy Bag Training

If you want to avoid a serious hand injury, be precise when hitting the heavy bag. Take your time when training and progressively build up your power.

Heavy Bag Bible

- Consider working out with music. Actually, your heavy bag workouts can be dramatically enhanced by training to music. It's my experience that training to fast, rhythmic music works wonders for conditioning training, while hard-driving aggressive rock music works best for proficiency and street training methods.

Book One: Heavy Bag Training

NOTES

Heavy Bag Bible

HEAVY BAG COMBINATIONS

The Ultimate Guide to Heavy Bag Punching Combinations

BOOK 2 OF A CONTINUING SERIES

SAMMY FRANCO

"The whole is greater than the sum of its parts."

- Aristotle

Book Two: Heavy Bag Combinations

Contents

About this book													135

Chapter 1: Beginner Combinations						137

Chapter 2: Intermediate Combinations					187

Chapter 3: Advanced Combinations						241

Chapter 4: Creating the Ultimate Heavy Bag Workout			295

Caution!

The author, publisher, and distributors of this book disclaim any liability from loss, injury, or damage, personal or otherwise, resulting from the information and procedures in this book. This book is for academic study only.

The information contained in this book is not designed to diagnose, treat, or manage any physical health conditions.

Before you begin any exercise or activity, including those suggested in this book, it is important to check with your physician to see if you have any condition that might be aggravated by strenuous training.

Book Two: Heavy Bag Combinations

About this book

Heavy Bag Combinations is my second book in the Heavy Bag Training Series. Practitioners who use this book as a reference tool will dramatically improve their heavy bag training skills. In fact, the punching combinations featured in this text will significantly improve your fighting skills, enhance your fitness and conditioning, and breathe new life into your current heavy bag workout sessions.

The heavy bag punching combinations featured in this book will also help you achieve maximum training performance in a variety of activities including, boxing (professional and amateur), mixed martial arts, kickboxing, self-defense, and personal fitness.

This book also provides step-by-step instructions for performing beginner, intermediate and advanced heavy bag combinations. Many experienced fighters will find these punching combinations very challenging. However, the best feature of this book is that it teaches you how to create an unlimited number of heavy bag workout programs filled with an infinite amount of unique punching combinations.

The heavy bag techniques featured in this book are based on my 30+ years of research, training and teaching the martial arts and combat sciences. I have taught these unique punching combinations to thousands of students, and I'm confident they will help you reach higher levels of training performance.

Heavy Bag Combinations has four chapters, each one covers a critical aspect of training. This book assumes you currently possess the basic punching skills. However, for those of you who need a quick refresher course, I have provided step-by-step instructions for all of the punching techniques in the appendix of this book. In addition, you will also find a glossary of terms. Since this is both a skill-building workbook and training guide, feel free to write in the margins, underline passages, and dog-ear the pages.

Finally, I encourage you to read this book from beginning to end, chapter by chapter. Only after you have read the entire book should you treat it as a reference and skip around, reading those chapters or combinations that directly apply to you.

Train hard!

- *Sammy Franco*

Book Two: Heavy Bag Combinations

Chapter 1
Beginner Combinations

Understanding Combination Punching

Since this book is devoted strictly to punching combinations, it's important for you to have a very clear understanding of its meaning. A combination or "compound attack" is the logical sequence of two or more techniques thrown in strategic succession. For example, a jab followed by a rear cross is considered to be a basic punching combination.

Unlimited Number of Combinations

Besides the actual body mechanics of punching, there are several other elements that comprise a punching combination. They include attack rhythms, height variations, the cadence of delivery, and practitioner movement. However, these are vast topics and must be reserved for future books. Nevertheless, when you combine and manipulate all of these elements you truly have an infinite amount of punching combinations that you can perform on the heavy bag.

When reading the combination sequence on the following pages, please note that the word "high" indicates punches delivered at head level while "low" represents punches delivered to the stomach level on the bag.

Once again, this book assumes you can perform the basic punching skills, including the jab, rear cross, hook and uppercut. However, if you are not familiar with these foundational punching techniques, please see the step-by-step instructions featured in the appendix of this book. Let's begin with beginner level punching combinations.

Book Two: Heavy Bag Combinations

Combination #1: jab-jab (all high)

Step 1: Begin from a fighting stance.

Step 2: Extend your lead arm forward and jab the bag.

139

Heavy Bag Bible

Step 3: Return to the stance position.

Step 4: Jab again at the bag.

Book Two: Heavy Bag Combinations

Combination #2: jab-jab (all low)

Step 1: Begin from a fighting stance.

Step 2: Bend your knees while snapping your lead arm at the bag.

141

Heavy Bag Bible

Step 3: Return to a low stance position.

Step 4: Again, bend your knees and jab low at the bag.

Book Two: Heavy Bag Combinations

Combination #3: jab-jab (high-low)

Step 1: Begin from a fighting stance.

Step 2: Jab high at the bag.

143

Heavy Bag Bible

Step 3: Return to a low stance position.

Step 4: Jab low at the bag.

Book Two: Heavy Bag Combinations

Combination #4: jab-jab (low-high)

Step 1: Begin from a fighting stance.

Step 2: Bend your knees and jab low at the bag.

Heavy Bag Bible

Step 3: Return to a low stance position.

Step 4: Quickly shoot up and jab high at the bag.

Book Two: Heavy Bag Combinations

Combination #5: jab-rear cross (all high)

Step 1: Begin from a fighting stance.

Step 2: Jab high at the bag.

147

Heavy Bag Bible

Step 3: Next, deliver a rear cross to the top of the bag.

Step 4: Return to the stance position

Book Two: Heavy Bag Combinations

Combination #6: jab-rear cross (high-low)

Step 1: Begin from a fighting stance.

Step 2: Jab high at the bag.

149

Heavy Bag Bible

Step 3: Next, deliver a low rear cross.

Step 4: Return to your stance.

150

Book Two: Heavy Bag Combinations

Combination #7: rear cross-jab (all high)

Step 1: Begin from a fighting stance.

Step 2: Next, deliver a high rear cross.

Heavy Bag Bible

Step 3: Jab high at the bag.

Step 4: Return to your stance.

Book Two: Heavy Bag Combinations

Combination #8: jab-rear cross-rear cross (all high)

Step 1: Begin from a fighting stance.

Step 2: Jab high at the bag.

153

Heavy Bag Bible

Step 3: Next, deliver a rear cross to the top of the bag.

Step 4: Return to your stance.

Book Two: Heavy Bag Combinations

Step 5: Deliver another rear cross.

Step 6: Return to your stance.

155

Heavy Bag Bible

Combination #9: rear cross-jab-rear cross-jab (all high)

Step 1: Start from a fighting stance.

Step 2: Deliver a rear cross to the top of the bag.

Book Two: Heavy Bag Combinations

Step 3: Jab high at the bag.

Step 4: Fire off a second rear cross.

Heavy Bag Bible

Step 5: Jab again at the bag.

Step 6: Return to the stance position.

Book Two: Heavy Bag Combinations

Combination #10: jab-jab-rear cross (all high)

Step 1: Begin from a fighting stance.

Step 2: Jab high at the bag.

159

Heavy Bag Bible

Step 3: Return to the stance position.

Step 4: Jab again at the bag.

Book Two: Heavy Bag Combinations

Step 5: Next, follow up with a rear cross to the top of the bag.

Step 6: Return to the stance position.

161

Heavy Bag Bible

Combination #11: jab-jab-rear cross (high-high-low)

Step 1: Start from a fighting stance.

Step 2: Throw a high jab at the bag.

Book Two: Heavy Bag Combinations

Step 3: Return to the stance position.

Step 4: Jab again at the bag.

Heavy Bag Bible

Step 5: Next, deliver a low rear cross at the bag.

Step 6: Return to your stance.

Book Two: Heavy Bag Combinations

Combination #12: jab-rear cross-jab (all high)

Step 1: Begin from a fighting stance.

Step 2: Jab high at the bag.

165

Heavy Bag Bible

Step 3: Next, deliver a rear cross to the top of the bag.

Step 4: Follow up with another high jab.

Book Two: Heavy Bag Combinations

Combination #13: jab-rear cross-jab (high-low-high)

Step 1: Begin from a fighting stance.

Step 2: Jab high at the bag.

Heavy Bag Bible

Step 3: Next, deliver a rear cross punch to the lower portion of the bag.

Step 4: Follow up with another high jab.

Book Two: Heavy Bag Combinations

Combination #14: jab-rear cross-jab-rear cross (all high)

Step 1: Begin from a fighting stance.

Step 2: Jab high at the bag.

Heavy Bag Bible

Step 3: Next, deliver a rear cross to the top of the bag.

Step 4: Follow up with another high jab.

Book Two: Heavy Bag Combinations

Step 5: Deliver another high rear cross.

Step 6: Return to your stance.

Heavy Bag Bible

Combination #15: jab-rear cross-jab-rear cross (high-low-high-low)

Step 1: Begin from a fighting stance.

Step 2: Jab high at the bag.

Book Two: Heavy Bag Combinations

Step 3: Next, deliver a low rear cross.

Step 4: Throw another high jab.

Heavy Bag Bible

Step 5: Follow up with another low rear cross.

Step 6: Return to the stance position.

Book Two: Heavy Bag Combinations

Combination #16: jab-rear cross-jab-rear cross (low-high-low-high)

Step 1: Begin from a fighting stance.

Step 2: Throw a low jab to the bag.

Heavy Bag Bible

Step 3: Next, a high rear cross.

Step 4: Follow up with another low jab.

Book Two: Heavy Bag Combinations

Step 5: Finish off with a high rear cross..

Step 6: Return to the stance position.

Heavy Bag Bible

Combination #17: jab-rear cross-jab-rear cross (all low)

Step 1: Begin from a fighting stance.

Step 2: Deliver a low jab at the bag.

Book Two: Heavy Bag Combinations

Step 3: Next, a low rear cross.

Step 4: Follow up with another low jab.

179

Heavy Bag Bible

Step 5: Finish off with a low rear cross.

Step 6: Return to the fighting stance.

Book Two: Heavy Bag Combinations

Combination #18: jab-jab-rear cross (low-low-high)

Step 1: Begin from a fighting stance.

Step 2: Throw a low jab at the bag.

181

Heavy Bag Bible

Step 3: Return to a low stance position.

Step 4: Throw another low jab.

182

Book Two: Heavy Bag Combinations

Step 5: Follow with a rear cross to the top of the bag.

Step 6: Return to the stance position.

Heavy Bag Bible

Combination #19: jab-jab-jab (high-low-high)

Step 1: Begin from a fighting stance.

Step 2: Jab high at the bag.

Book Two: Heavy Bag Combinations

Step 3: Return to a low stance position.

Step 4: Jab low at the bag.

Heavy Bag Bible

Step 5: Jab high at the bag.

Step 6: Return to the stance position.

Book Two: Heavy Bag Combinations

Chapter 2
Intermediate Combinations

Adding Hooks to Your Combinations

In this chapter, we are going to build off the combinations from the previous chapter and add circular punches to your heavy bag workout. More specifically, you're going to add hook punches to your punching combinations.

The hook punch is a devastating blow delivered from both the lead and rear side of the body. However, it's also one of the most difficult to master. To execute the hook punch correctly, you must maintain the correct wrist, forearm, and shoulder alignment. When delivering the punch, be sure your arm is bent at least 90 degrees and that your wrist and forearm are kept straight throughout the movement.

To execute the hook punch, quickly and smoothly raise your elbow up so that your arm is parallel to the ground while simultaneously torquing your shoulder, hip, and foot in the direction of the blow. As you throw the punch, be sure that your fist is positioned vertically. Never place your fist horizontally when throwing a hook. This inferior hand placement can cause a sprained or broken wrist. Avoid chambering or cocking the arm and excessive follow-through.

If you require more information about performing the hook punch, please see the appendix of this book.

Book Two: Heavy Bag Combinations

Combination #20: jab-rear cross-hook (all high)

Step 1: Begin from a fighting stance.

Step 2: Throw a high jab at the bag.

189

Heavy Bag Bible

Step 3: Next, deliver a high rear cross.

Step 4: Immediately follow with a lead hook punch.

Book Two: Heavy Bag Combinations

Combination #21: jab-rear cross-hook (high-high-low)

Step 1: Begin from a fighting stance.

Step 2: Extend you lead arm forward and jab the bag.

Heavy Bag Bible

Step 3: Next, deliver a rear cross.

Step 4: Immediately follow with a low lead hook punch.

Book Two: Heavy Bag Combinations

Combination #22: jab-rear cross-hook-hook (all high)

Step 1: Begin from a fighting stance.

Step 2: Extend your lead arm forward and jab the bag.

Heavy Bag Bible

Step 3: Next, deliver a rear cross to the top of the bag.

Step 4: Immediately follow with a lead hook punch.

Book Two: Heavy Bag Combinations

Step 5: Next, deliver a rear hook.

Step 6: Return to your stance.

Heavy Bag Bible

Combination #23: jab-rear cross-hook-hook (high-high-high-low)

Step 1: Begin from a fighting stance.

Step 2: Jab the bag.

Book Two: Heavy Bag Combinations

Step 3: Next, deliver a rear cross.

Step 4: Immediately follow with a lead hook.

Heavy Bag Bible

Step 5: Next, a low rear hook.

Step 6: Return to the fighting stance.

198

Book Two: Heavy Bag Combinations

Combination #24: jab-rear cross-hook-hook (high-high-low-high)

Step 1: Begin from a fighting stance.

Step 2: Jab the bag.

199

Heavy Bag Bible

Step 3: Next, deliver a rear cross.

Step 4: Immediately follow with a low lead hook punch.

Book Two: Heavy Bag Combinations

Step 5: Deliver a rear hook punch.

Step 6: Return to the stance position.

201

Combination #25: jab-rear hook-rear hook (high-high-low)

Step 1: Start from a fighting stance.

Step 2: Jab high at the bag.

Book Two: Heavy Bag Combinations

Step 3: Next, deliver a high rear hook.

Step 4: Follow with a low rear hook.

Heavy Bag Bible

Combination #26: jab-rear hook-rear hook (high-low-high)

Step 1: Begin from a fighting stance.

Step 2: Jab high at the bag.

Book Two: Heavy Bag Combinations

Step 3: Next, deliver a low rear hook.

Step 4: Follow with a high rear hook punch.

Heavy Bag Bible

Combination #27: jab-lead hook-rear cross (all high)

Step 1: Begin from a fighting stance.

Step 2: Jab high at the bag.

Book Two: Heavy Bag Combinations

Step 3: From the same arm, deliver a high lead hook.

Step 4: Next, throw a rear cross.

Combination #28: jab-lead hook-rear cross (low-low-high)

Step 1: Begin from a fighting stance.

Step 2: Jab low at the bag.

Book Two: Heavy Bag Combinations

Step 3: Next, deliver a low lead hook.

Step 4: Follow up with a rear cross.

Heavy Bag Bible

Combination #29: jab-lead hook-rear hook (all high)

Step 1: Begin from a fighting stance.

Step 2: Jab high at the bag.

Book Two: Heavy Bag Combinations

Step 3: Next, from the same arm, deliver a high lead hook.

Step 4: Follow up with a high rear hook.

Heavy Bag Bible

Combination #30: jab-lead hook-rear cross-lead hook (all high)

Step 1: Begin from a fighting stance.

Step 2: Jab high at the bag.

Book Two: Heavy Bag Combinations

Step 3: Next, from the same arm, deliver a high lead hook.

Step 4: Follow up with a rear cross.

Heavy Bag Bible

Step 5: A high lead hook.

Step 6: Return to the stance position.

Book Two: Heavy Bag Combinations

Combination #31: jab-lead hook-rear hook (high-low-low)

Step 1: Begin from a fighting stance.

Step 2: Jab high at the bag.

215

Heavy Bag Bible

Step 3: Next, deliver a low lead hook.

Step 4: Follow up with a low rear hook.

216

Book Two: Heavy Bag Combinations

Combination #32: jab-lead hook-rear hook (high-high-low)

Step 1: Begin from a fighting stance.

Step 2: Jab high at the bag.

Step 3: Next, from the same arm, deliver a high lead hook.

Step 4: Follow up with a low rear hook.

Book Two: Heavy Bag Combinations

Combination #33: jab-lead hook-rear hook (high-low-high)

Step 1: Begin from a fighting stance.

Step 2: Jab high at the bag.

219

Heavy Bag Bible

Step 3: Next, deliver a low lead hook.

Step 4: Follow up with a high rear hook.

Book Two: Heavy Bag Combinations

Combination #34: jab-jab-rear cross-lead hook (all high)

Step 1: Begin from a fighting stance.

Step 2: Jab high at the bag.

Heavy Bag Bible

Step 3: Quickly retract your punch.

Step 4: Follow up with another high jab.

Book Two: Heavy Bag Combinations

Step 5: Next, throw a high rear cross.

Step 6: A high lead hook completes the compound attack.

Heavy Bag Bible

Combination #35: jab-jab-rear cross-lead hook (high-high-high-low)

Step 1: Begin from a fighting stance.

Step 2: Jab high at the bag.

Book Two: Heavy Bag Combinations

Step 3: Quickly retract your punch.

Step 4: Follow up with another high jab.

Heavy Bag Bible

Step 5: Next, throw a high rear cross.

Step 6: A low lead hook completes the compound attack.

Book Two: Heavy Bag Combinations

Combination #36: rear cross-lead hook-lead hook-rear hook (low-high-high-low)

Step 1: Begin from a fighting stance.

Step 2: Deliver a low rear cross at the bag.

Heavy Bag Bible

Step 3: Next, a high lead hook.

Step 4: Quickly retract your punch.

Book Two: Heavy Bag Combinations

Step 5: Throw another high lead hook at the bag.

Step 6: Finish with a low rear hook.

229

Heavy Bag Bible

Combination #37: rear cross-lead hook-lead hook-rear hook (high-low-low-high)

Step 1: Begin from a fighting stance.

Step 2: Throw a high rear cross.

Book Two: Heavy Bag Combinations

Step 3: Next, a low lead hook.

Step 4: Return to a low stance position.

Heavy Bag Bible

Step 5: Deliver another low lead hook to the bag.

Step 6: Finish with a high rear hook.

Book Two: Heavy Bag Combinations

Combination 38: rear cross-lead hook-rear cross-lead hook-rear hook (high-high-low-high-low)

Step 1: Begin from a fighting stance.

Step 2: Throw a high rear cross.

Heavy Bag Bible

Step 3: Next, a high lead hook at the bag.

Step 4: Follow with a low rear cross.

Book Two: Heavy Bag Combinations

Step 5: Deliver another lead hook.

Step 6: Finish with a low rear hook.

235

Heavy Bag Bible

Combination 39: rear cross-rear hook-rear hook-lead hook-lead hook (high-high-low-low-low)

Step 1: Begin from a fighting stance.

Step 2: Throw a high rear cross.

236

Book Two: Heavy Bag Combinations

Step 3: Next, a high rear hook.

Step 4: Deliver a low rear hook.

Step 5: Follow with a low lead hook to the bag.

Step 6: Return to a low stance position.

Book Two: Heavy Bag Combinations

Step 7: Fire off another low lead hook.

Step 8: Return to your fighting stance.

239

Book Two: Heavy Bag Combinations

Chapter 3
Advanced Combinations

Adding Uppercuts to Your Combinations

In this chapter, we are going to build off the combinations from the previous two chapters and add uppercuts to your heavy bag combinations. The uppercut is an explosive and powerful close-quarter punch that travels in a vertical trajectory to its target. Uppercuts can also be delivered from either your lead or rear arm.

To execute the uppercut, quickly twist and lift your body in the direction of the blow. Make sure that the punch has a short arc and that you avoid any "winding up" motions. A properly executed uppercut should feel like an explosive jolt.

Once again, if you require more information about performing the uppercut, please see the appendix of this book.

Book Two: Heavy Bag Combinations

Combination #40: jab-jab-rear uppercut (all high)

Step 1: Begin from a fighting stance.

Step 2: Jab high at the bag.

243

Heavy Bag Bible

Step 3: Quickly retract your punch.

Step 4: Jab again at the bag.

Book Two: Heavy Bag Combinations

Step 5: Next, throw a rear uppercut.

Step 6: Return to your fighting stance.

Heavy Bag Bible

Combination #41: jab-lead uppercut-rear cross (all high)

Step 1: Begin from a fighting stance.

Step 2: Jab high at the bag.

Book Two: Heavy Bag Combinations

Step 3: Next, throw a lead uppercut.

Step 4: Follow up with a rear cross.

Heavy Bag Bible

Combination #42: jab-lead uppercut-rear cross (low-high-low)

Step 1: Begin from a fighting stance.

Step 2: Jab low at the bag.

Book Two: Heavy Bag Combinations

Step 3: Next, throw a lead uppercut.

Step 4: Finish with a low rear cross.

Combination #43: jab-rear uppercut-lead uppercut (all high)

Step 1: Begin from a fighting stance.

Step 2: Jab high at the bag.

250

Book Two: Heavy Bag Combinations

Step 3: Next, throw a rear uppercut.

Step 4: Finish with a lead uppercut.

Heavy Bag Bible

Combination 44: jab-rear uppercut-lead uppercut-rear cross-lead hook (all high)

Step 1: Begin from a fighting stance.

Step 2: Jab high at the bag.

252

Book Two: Heavy Bag Combinations

Step 3: Next, throw a rear uppercut.

Step 4: Follow up with a lead uppercut.

Heavy Bag Bible

Step 5: Deliver a high rear cross.

Step 6: Finish with a high lead hook.

Book Two: Heavy Bag Combinations

Combination #45: jab-rear cross-lead hook-rear uppercut (all high)

Step 1: Begin from a fighting stance.

Step 2: Jab high at the bag.

255

Step 3: Next, a high lead hook.

Step 4: Finish with a rear uppercut.

Book Two: Heavy Bag Combinations

Combination #46: jab-rear cross-lead hook-rear cross (all high)

Step 1: Begin from a fighting stance.

Step 2: Jab high at the bag.

257

Step 3: Throw a high rear cross.

Step 4: Next, a high lead hook.

Book Two: Heavy Bag Combinations

Step 5: Another high rear cross.

Step 6: Return to your fighting stance.

Heavy Bag Bible

Combination #47: jab-rear cross-lead hook-rear cross-lead hook-lead hook (5x high-1 low)

Step 1: Begin from a fighting stance.

Step 2: Jab high at the bag.

260

Book Two: Heavy Bag Combinations

Step 3: Throw a high rear cross.

Step 4: Next, a high lead hook.

Heavy Bag Bible

Step 5: A high rear cross.

Step 6: A high lead hook.

262

Book Two: Heavy Bag Combinations

Step 7: A low lead hook.

Step 8: Return to your fighting stance.

263

Combination #48: rear cross-jab-rear hook (all high)

Step 1: Begin from a fighting stance.

Step 2: Throw a high rear cross.

Book Two: Heavy Bag Combinations

Step 3: Jab high at the bag.

Step 4: Follow up with a high rear hook.

Combination #49: rear cross-jab-rear hook-lead uppercut-lead hook (high-high-low-high-high)

Step 1: Begin from a fighting stance.

Step 2: Throw a high rear cross.

Book Two: Heavy Bag Combinations

Step 3: Jab high at the bag.

Step 4: Next, a low rear hook.

Heavy Bag Bible

Step 5: Follow up with a lead uppercut.

Step 6: Finish with a high lead hook.

Book Two: Heavy Bag Combinations

Combination #50: rear cross-lead hook-rear cross-lead hook-rear uppercut (high-high-high-low-high)

Step 1: Begin from a fighting stance.

Step 2: Throw a high rear cross.

Heavy Bag Bible

Step 3: Next, a high lead hook.

Step 4: Another rear cross.

Book Two: Heavy Bag Combinations

Step 5: A low lead hook.

Step 6: Finish with a rear uppercut.

Heavy Bag Bible

Combination #51: rear hook-lead hook-rear hook-lead uppercut (all high)

Step 1: Begin from a fighting stance.

Step 2: Throw a high rear hook.

Book Two: Heavy Bag Combinations

Step 3: Next a high lead hook.

Step 4: Follow up with a high rear hook.

Heavy Bag Bible

Step 5: Next, a lead uppercut.

Step 6: Return to your fighting stance.

Book Two: Heavy Bag Combinations

Combination #52: rear hook-lead hook-rear hook-lead hook-rear uppercut (high-low-low-low-high)

Step 1: Begin from a fighting stance.

Step 2: Throw a high rear hook.

275

Step 3: Next, a low lead hook.

Step 4: Follow up with a low rear hook.

Book Two: Heavy Bag Combinations

Step 5: Deliver another low lead hook.

Step 6: Finish with a rear uppercut.

Heavy Bag Bible

Combination #53: rear uppercut-lead uppercut-rear hook-lead hook (all high)

Step 1: Begin from a fighting stance.

Step 2: Throw a rear uppercut.

Book Two: Heavy Bag Combinations

Step 3: Next, a lead uppercut.

Step 4: Follow with a high rear hook.

Heavy Bag Bible

Step 5: Next, a high lead hook.

Step 6: Return to your fighting stance.

Book Two: Heavy Bag Combinations

Combination #54: rear uppercut-lead uppercut-rear uppercut-lead uppercut (all high)

Step 1: Begin from a fighting stance.

Step 2: Throw a rear uppercut.

Heavy Bag Bible

Step 3: Follow up with a lead uppercut.

Step 4: Deliver another rear uppercut.

Book Two: Heavy Bag Combinations

Step 5: Throw a final lead uppercut.

Step 6: Return to a fighting stance.

Heavy Bag Bible

Combination #55: lead uppercut-rear uppercut-lead uppercut-rear uppercut-lead hook-lead hook-rear hook

Step 1: Begin from a fighting stance.

Step 2: Throw a lead uppercut.

Book Two: Heavy Bag Combinations

Step 3: Next, a rear uppercut.

Step 4: Follow up with a lead uppercut.

Heavy Bag Bible

Step 5: A high rear hook.

Step 6: Next, a high lead hook.

Book Two: Heavy Bag Combinations

Step 7: Deliver a high rear hook.

Step 8: Return to a fighting stance.

Heavy Bag Bible

Combination #56: rear uppercut-lead hook-rear hook-lead uppercut-lead hook (all high)

Step 1: Begin from a fighting stance.

Step 2: Deliver a rear uppercut.

Book Two: Heavy Bag Combinations

Step 3: Next, a high lead hook.

Step 4: Throw a high rear hook.

Heavy Bag Bible

Step 5: Follow with a lead uppercut.

Step 6: Next, a high lead hook.

Book Two: Heavy Bag Combinations

Combination #57: jab-rear cross-lead & rear hooks-lead & rear uppercuts (all high)

Step 1: Begin from a fighting stance.

Step 2: Jab high at the bag.

Heavy Bag Bible

Step 3: Throw a high rear cross.

Step 4: Next, a high lead hook.

292

Book Two: Heavy Bag Combinations

Step 5: Deliver a high rear hook.

Step 6: A lead uppercut.

Heavy Bag Bible

Step 7: Follow with a rear uppercut.

Step 8: Return to your fighting stance.

Book Two: Heavy Bag Combinations

Chapter 4
Creating the Ultimate Heavy Bag Workout

Time-Based Heavy Bag Training

In my first book, *Heavy Bag Training*, I discussed the importance of creating time-based heavy bag workouts. Essentially, a time-based heavy bag workout is predicated on "rounds" and it's the best way to organize your workout. Before you begin, however, you need to decide on the duration of your heavy bag rounds as well as the rest intervals.

For example, mixed martial artists, boxers and kickboxers will often hit the heavy bag for three-minute rounds and then rest for a one-minute period. Depending on their level of conditioning and specific training goals, they might do this for a total of five to eight rounds.

Initially, you'll need to experiment with both the round duration and rest intervals to see what works best for you. Remember to start off slow and progressively build up the intensity and duration of your workouts.

To get you started on the right track, I have included some sample time-based workouts you might want to try. Keep in mind, the advanced level workouts are for elite athletes who have a minimum of five years of heavy bag training.

Sample Time Based Heavy Bag Workouts

Skill Level	Duration of Each Round	Rest Period	Total Number of rounds
Beginner	1 minute	2 minutes	3
Beginner	1 minute	1 minute	3
Beginner	2 minutes	2 minute	3
Beginner	2 minutes	1 minute	3
Intermediate	3 minutes	2 minutes	5
Intermediate	3 minutes	1 minute	5
Intermediate	3 minutes	2 minute	6
Intermediate	3 minutes	1 minute	6
Advanced	4 minutes	2 minutes	8
Advanced	4 minutes	1 minute	8
Advanced	5 minutes	2 minutes	10
Advanced	5 minutes	1 minute	10

A Word of Caution Before you Start Training!

Take your time when working out on the bag. If you are learning how to use the heavy bag for the very first time, I strongly urge you to take your time and develop the proper punching body mechanics before tearing into the bag.

Remember, the heavy bag is a serious piece of training equipment and it's easy to get injured when using it. Heavy bag workouts are also tough and very demanding on the body. Avoid premature exhaustion by pacing yourself during your workouts. Remember, it's not a race! Enjoy the process of learning how to use the bag with skill and finesse.

Warning! Before you begin any exercise program, including those suggested in this book, it is important to check with your physician to see if you have any condition that might be aggravated by strenuous exercise.

The Art of Combination Blending

All of the punching combinations featured in this book are both foundational and challenging and will keep you busy for many years to come. In fact, you can make significant progress by sticking with the basic combinations featured in each chapter and just performing them over and over again for the duration of your round.

However, for those of you who require a greater challenge in your heavy bag training, you can perform *"combination blending."* Essentially, combination blending is strategically combining two heavy bag combinations into one seamless combination duration a training round.

For example, if you are a beginner, you would pick two combination sequences from *Chapter 1: (Beginner Combinations)* of this book. For instance, you might pick combination #3 and combination #13.

- **Combination #3: jab-jab (high-low)**
- **Combination #13: jab-rear cross-jab (high-low-high)**

Next, you would combine the two punching sequences and perform them on the heavy bag for the duration of a three minute round. The entire combination sequence would look like the following:

Book Two: Heavy Bag Combinations

Combination Blending Example: Combination 3+13= jab-jab (high-low)-jab-rear cross-jab (high-low-high)

Step 1: Begin from a fighting stance.

Step 2: Jab high at the bag.

Step 3: Return to a low stance position.

Step 4: Jab low at the bag.

Book Two: Heavy Bag Combinations

Step 5: Jab high at the bag.

Step 6: Next, deliver a low rear cross at the bag.

Heavy Bag Bible

Step 7: Follow up with another high jab.

Step 8: Return to your stance.

Book Two: Heavy Bag Combinations

Here is another example of combination blending. However, this time we are going to blend combinations for an advanced practitioner. Again, this requires you to pick at least two combination sequences from *Chapter 3: (Advanced Combinations)* of this book. For instance, you might pick combination #42 and combination #48.

- **Combination #42: jab-lead uppercut-rear cross (low-high-low)**
- **Combination #48: rear cross-jab-rear hook (all high)**

Next, you would combine the two sequences and perform them on the heavy bag for the duration of your round. This sequence would look like the following:

- **Combination 42+48 = jab-lead uppercut-rear cross (low-high-low)+rear cross-jab-rear hook (all high)**

Combination 42+48 = jab-lead uppercut-rear cross (low-high-low)+rear cross-jab-rear hook (all high)

Step 1: Begin from a fighting stance.

303

Heavy Bag Bible

Step 2: Jab low at the bag.

Step 3: Throw a lead uppercut.

Book Two: Heavy Bag Combinations

Step 4: Next, a low rear cross.

Step 5: Follow with a high rear cross.

Step 6: Deliver a high jab.

Step 7: Finish with high rear hook.

Book Two: Heavy Bag Combinations

Is Combination Blending Necessary?

Some of you might be wondering if combination blending is necessary for heavy bag training? Or if some of the combination sequences are too lengthy for practical punching applications. After all, how many punches does one really need for an effective compound attack? Well, the answer to these questions really depends on the individual and their personal training goals. Nevertheless, I've included combination blending in this book for some of the following important reasons:

1. It generates a truly unlimited supply of heavy bag combinations that will literally challenge you for a lifetime.
2. It prevents your workout routines from becoming boring, stagnant, and monotonous.
3. It's a great mental toughness exercise that develops important attributes like attention control, instrumental aggression, immediate resilience, and self-confidence.

Reversing the Combination Blending Sequence

Combination blending is the most challenging form of heavy bag training. Like I stated earlier, when used correctly, you can create an infinite amount of punching combinations that will challenge you for the rest of your life!

Moreover, you can also reverse the sequence of the blended combination. For instance, the kinesthetic feel and strategic application of punching sequence 42+48 will be substantially different from 48+42. If you don't believe me, try it out on the heavy bag and see for yourself.

Combination Blending Tips

It's important not to exceed your skill level when performing combination blending. For example, if you're a beginner, never integrate advanced or intermediate combinations into your heavy bag workout. Be patient and stick to guidelines outlined in this book.

However, intermediate practitioners are encouraged to integrate beginner level combinations with combination blending. Likewise, advanced practitioners may add beginner and intermediate punching combinations with advanced combinations. Please refer to the accompanying chart for more information.

For your convenience, I have also provided several combination blending samples for beginner, intermediate, and advanced levels of training. Again, these are just examples of what you can do in your training.

Book Two: Heavy Bag Combinations

Combination Blending Examples

	Beginner level	Intermediate level	Advanced level
Sequence	1+2	20+23	40+1
Sequence	1+3	25+27	42+25
Sequence	4+8	1+28	45+8
Sequence	4+12	11+31	5+50
Sequence	5+3	12+36	51+19
Sequence	6+9	19+34	54+6
Sequence	7+13	27+39	10+55
Sequence	8+5	33+20	48+12
Sequence	9+13	21+22	57+3
Sequence	10+14	35+17	47+29
Sequence	11+8	24+30	44+13
Sequence	14+1	26+2	49+58
Sequence	12+6	37+33	55+38
Sequence	15+17	39+19	53+12
Sequence	18+5	16+26	41+41

Punching Combination Review

For your convenience, I have provided a list of all of the punching combinations featured in each of the chapters.

Chapter 1: Beginner Combinations

1. jab-jab (all high)
2. jab-jab (all low)
3. jab-jab (high-low)
4. jab-jab (low-high)
5. jab-rear cross (all high)
6. jab-rear cross (high-low)
7. rear cross-jab (all high)
8. jab-rear cross-rear cross (all high)
9. rear cross-jab-rear cross-jab (all high)
10. jab-jab-rear cross (all high)
11. jab-jab-rear cross (high-high-low)
12. jab-rear cross-jab (all high)
13. jab-rear cross-jab (high-low-high)
14. jab-rear cross-jab-rear cross (all high)
15. jab-rear cross-jab-rear cross (high-low-high-low)
16. jab-rear cross-jab-rear cross (low-high-low-high)
17. jab-rear cross-jab-rear cross (all low)
18. jab-jab-rear cross (low-low-high)
19. jab-jab-jab (high-low-high)

Book Two: Heavy Bag Combinations

Chapter 2: Intermediate Combinations

20. jab-rear cross-hook (all high)
21. jab-rear cross-hook (high-high-low)
22. jab-rear cross-hook-hook (all high)
23. jab-rear cross-hook-hook (high-high-high-low)
24. jab-rear cross-hook-hook (high-high-low-high)
25. jab-rear hook-rear hook (high-high-low)
26. jab-rear hook-rear hook (high-low-high)
27. jab-lead hook-rear cross (all high)
28. jab-lead hook-rear cross (low-low-high)
29. jab-lead hook-rear hook (all high)
30. jab-lead hook-rear cross-lead hook (all high)
31. jab-lead hook-rear hook (high-low-low)
32. jab-lead hook-rear hook (high-high-low)
33. jab-lead hook-rear hook (high-low-high)
34. jab-jab-rear cross-lead hook (all high)
35. jab-jab-rear cross-lead hook (high-high-high-low)
36. rear cross-lead hook-lead hook-rear hook (low-high-high-low)
37. rear cross-lead hook-lead hook-rear hook (high-low-low-high)
38. rear cross-lead hook-rear cross-lead hook-rear hook (high-high-low-high-low)
39. rear cross-rear hook-rear hook-lead hook-lead hook (high-high-low-low-low)

Chapter 3: Advanced Combinations

40. jab-jab-rear uppercut (all high)
41. jab-lead uppercut-rear cross (all high)
42. jab-lead uppercut-rear cross (low-high-low)
43. jab-rear uppercut-lead uppercut (all high)
44. jab-rear uppercut-lead uppercut-rear cross-lead hook (all high)
45. jab-rear cross-lead hook-rear uppercut (all high)
46. jab-rear cross-lead hook-rear cross (all high)
47. jab-rear cross-lead hook-rear cross-lead hook-lead hook (5x high-1 low)
48. rear cross-jab-rear hook (all high)
49. rear cross-jab-rear hook-lead uppercut-lead hook (high-high-low-high-high)
50. rear cross-lead hook-rear cross-lead hook-rear uppercut (high-high-high-low-high)
51. rear hook-lead hook-rear hook-lead uppercut (all high)
52. rear hook-lead hook-rear hook-lead hook-rear uppercut (high-low-low-low-high)
53. rear uppercut-lead uppercut-rear hook-lead hook (all high)
54. rear uppercut-lead uppercut-rear uppercut-lead uppercut (all high)
55. lead uppercut-rear uppercut-lead uppercut-rear uppercut-lead hook-lead hook-rear hook
56. rear uppercut-lead hook-rear hook-lead uppercut-lead hook (all high)
57. jab-rear cross-lead & rear hooks-lead & rear uppercuts (all high)

Book Two: Heavy Bag Combinations

Create Your Own Punching Combinations

To get you into the creative process of developing punching combinations, I have provided a section for you to write down your own heavy bag combinations.

1.
2.
3.
4.
5.
6.
7.
8.
9.
10.
11.
12.
13.
14.
15.
16.
17.
18.

19.

20.

21.

22.

23.

24.

25.

26.

27.

28.

29.

30.

31.

32.

33.

34.

35.

36.

37.

38.

39.

40.

Book Two: Heavy Bag Combinations

You Need to Move Around the Bag

To ensure that you would clearly understand all of the principles featured in this book, I intentionally had every punching technique photographed from a stationary position.

However, when working out on the heavy bag, you should always move around. This concept is important for some of the following important reasons:

1. It increases the overall intensity of your heavy bag workout.
2. It amplifies the power of your punches.
3. It gives you a greater understanding and appreciation of fighting ranges.
4. It develops good fighting habits. For example, it makes you a more elusive target when fighting an actual opponent.

The following series of photographs demonstrate how to move around the heavy bag when throwing a series of punches.

Step 1: Begin with a high jab.

Heavy Bag Bible

Step 2: Jab again as you move clockwise around the bag.

Step 3: Throw a high rear hook at the bag.

Book Two: Heavy Bag Combinations

Step 4: As the bag swings, move clockwise again.

Step 5: Jab again.

Step 6: Jab low at the bag.

Step 7: Continue to move clockwise around the bag.

Book Two: Heavy Bag Combinations

Step 8: Jab high at the bag.

Step 9: Follow with a rear cross.

319

Heavy Bag Bible

Step 10: Throw a lead hook.

Step 11: Next, a rear hook punch.

Book Two: Heavy Bag Combinations

Step 12: Follow with a low lead hook.

Step 13: Continue to move clockwise and jab at the bag.

Heavy Bag Bible

Step 14: Next, throw a high rear hook.

Step 15: Jab low at the bag.

322

Book Two: Heavy Bag Combinations

Step 16: Follow up with a lead hook.

Step 17: As you complete a circle around the heavy bag, deliver one final jab.

NOTES

HEAVY BAG WORKOUT

A HARD-CORE GUIDE TO HEAVY BAG WORKOUT ROUTINES

BOOK 3 OF A CONTINUING SERIES

SAMMY FRANCO

"It is never too late to be what you might have been."

- George Eliot

Contents

ABOUT THIS BOOK	329
PRELIMINARY STUFF	331
THE WORKOUT ROUTINES	345
Conditioning Training	346
Proficiency Training	347
Street Training	348
Time-Based Training	350
Ambidextrous Training	355
Elevation Drill	362
Piston Punching	370
Cyclone Drill	376
Hit the Seam Drill	381
X-Training	388
Punch a Hole Exercise	394
Technique Isolation Training	402
Defensive Bag Training	409
Interval Training	432
Bare-Knuckle Training	453
Pummel Training	458
Impairment Training	466
HEAVY BAG RESOURCES	479
APPENDIX	481
GLOSSARY	493
ABOUT SAMMY FRANCO	525

Caution!

The author, publisher, and distributors of this book disclaim any liability from loss, injury, or damage, personal or otherwise, resulting from the information and procedures in this book. This book is for academic study only.

The information contained in this book is not designed to diagnose, treat, or manage any physical health conditions.

Before you begin any exercise or activity, including those suggested in this book, it is important to check with your physician to see if you have any condition that might be aggravated by strenuous training.

Book Three: Heavy Bag Workout

About this book

Heavy Bag Workout is my third book in the Heavy Bag Training Series. This comprehensive book features over two dozen "out of the box" workout routines that will maximize your fighting skills for boxing, mixed martial arts, kickboxing, self-defense, and personal fitness.

With over 100 detailed photographs and step-by-step instructions, Heavy Bag Workout has beginner, intermediate and advanced workout routines that will make you hit faster and harder than ever before!

This unique book provides step-by-step instructions for performing a wide range of beginner, intermediate and advanced heavy bag workout routines. Whether you're an elite fighter or a complete beginner, this comprehensive book will take your fighting skills to the next level and beyond!

The exercises featured in this book are based on my 30+ years of research, training and teaching the martial arts and combat sciences. I have taught these unique drills to thousands of my students, and I'm confident they will help you reach higher levels of performance.

This book assumes you currently possess the basic punching skills. However, for those of you who need a quick refresher course, I have provided step-by-step instructions for all of the punching techniques in the appendix of this book. In addition, you will also find a glossary of terms. Since this is both a skill-building workbook and training guide, feel free to write in the margins, underline passages, and dog-ear the pages.

Finally, I encourage you to read this book from beginning to end, chapter by chapter. Only after you have read the entire book should you treat it as a reference and skip around, reading those topics that directly apply to you.

Train hard!

- Sammy Franco

Book Three: Heavy Bag Workout

PRELIMINARY STUFF

Heavy Bag Refresher

Before we begin with the workout routines, it's important to go over a few important things. For some of you this information will be enlightening, for others it will serve as a good refresher. Regardless of your training experience, these fundamental concepts are timeless and will benefit anyone.

Benefits of Heavy Bag Training

As I discussed in *Volume 1* of this book series, *Heavy Bag Training: For Boxing, Mixed Martial Arts, and Self-Defense*, the heavy bag is a fantastic piece of training equipment that provides a full range of benefits for the practitioner. Some of these benefits include:

- Developing and sharpening your fighting skills.
- Conditioning your entire body for the rigors of intense fighting.
- Improving muscular endurance.
- Strengthening your bones, tendons, and ligaments.
- Conditioning your cardiovascular system.
- Relieving stress and channeling aggressive energy in a productive manner.
- Developing several mental toughness attributes, such as instrumental aggression, immediate resilience, self-confidence, and attention control.

Finding the Right Heavy Bag

The heavy bag is constructed of either top grain leather, canvas or vinyl. Most bags are 14 inches in diameter and 42 inches in length. The interior of the bag is filled with either cotton fiber, thick foam, sand or other durable material. Depending on the brand, heavy bags can weigh anywhere from seventy-five to two hundred and fifty pounds.

The Heavier, The Better!

The weight of the heavy bag is probably the most important consideration when making a purchase. As a rule of thumb, try to buy the heaviest bag you can afford. Remember, when it comes to heavy bag training, *the heavier, the better!* If possible, avoid buying a bag that weighs under 100 pounds. Anything lighter won't provide sufficient resistance against powerful punches. As a result, the bag will swing uncontrollably when working out. I use a 150-pound heavy bag in my training. It offers the ideal amount of resistance for intense power punching sessions.

When looking to buy a heavy bag, avoid purchasing it from your local sporting goods store, as most of these bags are cheap, poorly made, and won't provide years of reliable use. The heavy bag is a serious piece of training equipment, so you should spare no expense and look for the highest quality brand that you can afford.

The good news is you can find a reasonably priced quality bag on the Internet. Here are just a few reputable companies that stand by their products:

- **Ringside Equipment** (ringside.com)
- **Combat Sports, Inc** (combatsports.com)
- **Title Boxing** (titleboxing.com)
- **Everlast Equipment** (everlast.com)

Heavy Bag Bible

If possible, avoid purchasing a self-standing punching bag. While these "fitness bags" might look like a heavy bag, I can assure you they are not. In fact, these bags are poorly designed and cannot withstand the striking power of a heavy hitter.

The Best Places to Workout

Safe and effective heavy bag training will require you to find a place that will allow both you and the bag to move around freely. The location should also be a relatively quiet place that is free of distractions. Here are a few places you might want to consider:

- Garage
- Carport
- Basement
- Barn
- Home gym (if you are fortunate enough)
- Open field or backyard
- Warehouse
- Under a deck

Heavy Bag Gear

Before you begin working out, invest in a good pair of bag gloves that will protect your hands. When buying gloves, spare no expense and look for a high-quality brand. This will provide years of reliable use and will help ensure a better quality workout.

Bag gloves are constructed of either top grain cowhide or durable

vinyl. There are two styles of bag gloves sold on the market:
- *Mitt style gloves*
- *Finger style gloves*

If you don't think you'll need bag gloves, think again. Striking the heavy bag without hand protection causes sore knuckles, bruised bones, hand inflammation, sore wrists, and scraped knuckles. These minor injuries will set your training back for several weeks in order for your hands to heal. However, for those of you who are interested in bare-knuckle training, I discuss it in the next chapter.

Boxing Gloves

Boxing gloves can also be used for heavy bag training. In fact, boxing gloves are often used by advanced practitioners for developing arm strength and endurance.

The ideal boxing glove is one that provides comfort, protection, and durability. Depending on your training objective, the glove can weigh anywhere from ten to sixteen ounces.

Here are some important features to be aware of when purchasing a pair of boxing gloves:

- To avoid wrist injuries, the glove should fit snugly.
- The boxing glove should be composed of multi-layered foam padding.
- The glove should have a sufficient palm grip that provides comfort and fist stabilization.
- To avoid a thumb injury, the glove should have thumb-lock stitching.
- The glove should be double-stitched to ensure durability.
- The entire glove should be constructed of top-quality materials to increase its durability.

Heavy Bag Bible

- The glove should be relatively easy to slip-on and off your hands. Velcro fasteners are sometimes preferred over laces.

Hand Wraps

Hand Wraps (also called wrist wraps) are used by experienced athletes who want an added measure of protection to their hands and wrists when hitting the heavy bag. They provide support to the entire hand and wrist area and can help prevent osteoarthritis in later years.

Essentially, hand wraps are long strips of cloth measuring two inches wide and nine to eighteen feet long. The longer hand wraps are more often used by practitioners who have large hands and who wish to have greater hand protection. You can find hand wraps at most sporting goods stores as well as the Internet.

Hand wraps should only be used in conjunction with either large bag gloves or boxing gloves. Do not strike the heavy bag with just your hand wraps as this can easily injure your hands.

Hand wraps are washable and should be cleaned after every workout. Although there are many hand wrapping techniques, the procedures shown on page 7 is suggested.

While hand wraps are a necessary piece of training equipment for boxing and other combat sports, I don't recommend using them for self-defense training. Reality based self-defense training requires you to condition your hands to withstand bare-fisted striking.

Boxing gloves can also be used if your knuckles are too sore or bruised to hit the heavy bag. The extra padding can make all the difference between skipping a workout and sticking with your routine.

Book Three: Heavy Bag Workout

How to Apply Hand Wraps

How to wrap your hands and wrists with hand wraps. Follow steps A through P.

Interval Workout Timer

Since heavy bag training is structured around time and rounds, you should invest in a good workout timer. Boxers, mixed martial artists, and kickboxers will use workout timers to keep track of their time during their rounds.

Most workout timers will allow you to adjust your round lengths anywhere from 30 seconds to 9 minutes. Rest time can be set from 30 seconds to 5 minutes depending on your level of conditioning and training goals.

There are several professional timers sold on the market, and they vary in price. Be forewarned! Some of them can be very pricey. However, there are numerous smartphone apps that replicate the same function and characteristics of an actual interval timer. These workout timer apps are convenient and very inexpensive. Your best bet is to search the Internet or your favorite app store for one that meets your specific needs.

Workout Timers are great for:

- Keeping track of the number of rounds and the time of each round.
- Measuring your current level of cardiovascular conditioning.
- Monitoring your progress in your heavy bag training.
- Creating healthy competition in your heavy bag routine.

Important Training Tips

Here are some important tips when working out on the bag:
1. Always warm up with some light stretching and calisthenics before working out.
2. Gradually build up the force of your blows. Remember, a beginner's wrists are too weak to accommodate full-force punches.

Book Three: Heavy Bag Workout

3. Never sacrifice your balance for power.
4. Remember to snap your punches.
5. Always keep your wrists straight when striking the bag.
6. Always maintain proper form.
7. Move around and avoid remaining stationary.
8. Learn to blend your strikes into logical combinations.
9. Pace yourself to avoid premature exhaustion.
10. Don't wear jewelry or a watch when training.
11. Stay relaxed and avoid unnecessary muscular tension.
12. Never hold your breath. Remember to exhale with the delivery of each and every technique.
13. Avoid the urge to stop the bag from moving. Let it swing freely!
14. If you don't know the proper way to throw a punch or kick, get instruction from a qualified coach or instructor.
15. Avoid heavy bag training two days in a row. Give your body a few days to recover from your last workout.

You are never too old for heavy bag training.

Heavy Bag Bible

Get a Check-Up First

Heavy Bag training is extremely intense and very taxing on your heart. So, before you begin any exercise program, including those suggested in this book, it is important to check with your doctor to see if you have any condition that might be aggravated by this type of strenuous exercise.

Warming Up

Before beginning any of the drills, it's important that you first warm up and stretch out. Warming up slowly increases the internal temperature of your body while stretching improves your workout performance, keeps you flexible, and helps reduce the possibility of an injury.

Some of the best exercises for warming up are jumping jacks, rope skipping or a short jog before training. Another effective method of warming up your muscles is to perform light and easy movements with the weights.

When stretching out, keep in mind that all movements should be performed in a slow and controlled manner. Try to hold your stretch for a minimum of sixty seconds and avoid all bouncing movements. You should feel mild tension on the muscle that is being stretched. Remember to stay relaxed and focus on what you are doing. Here are seven stretches to get you started.

- **Neck stretch** - from a comfortable standing position, slowly tilt your head to the right side of your neck, holding it for

Book Three: Heavy Bag Workout

a count of twenty. Then tilt your head to the left side for approximately twenty seconds. Stretch each side of the neck at least three times.

- **Triceps stretch** - from a standing position, keep your knees slightly bent, extend your right arm overhead, hold the elbow of your right arm with your left hand, and slowly pull your right elbow to the left. Keep your hips straight as you stretch your triceps gently for thirty seconds. Repeat this stretch for the other arm.
- **Hamstring stretch** - from a seated position on the floor, extend your right leg in front of you with your toe pointing to the ceiling. Place the sole of your left foot in the inside of your extended leg. Gently lean forward at the hips and stretch out the hamstrings of your right leg. Hold this position for a minimum of sixty seconds. Switch legs and repeat the stretch.
- **Spinal twist** - from a seated position on the floor, extend your right leg in front of you. Raise your left leg and place it on the outside of your right leg. Place your right elbow on the outside of your left thigh. Stabilize your stretch with your elbow and twist your upper body and head to your left side. Breathe naturally and hold this stretch for a minimum of thirty seconds. Switch legs and repeat this stretch for the other side.
- **Quad stretch** - assume a sitting position on the floor with your hamstrings folded and resting on top of your calves. Your

You need a good stretching program designed to loosen up every muscle group. Remember, you can't kick or punch, or otherwise execute the necessary body mechanics if you're "tight" or inflexible. Stretching on a regular basis will also increase the muscles' range of motion, improve circulation, reduce the possibility of injury, and relieve daily stress.

toes should be pointed behind you, and your instep should be flush with the ground. Sit comfortably into the stretch and hold for a minimum of sixty seconds.
- **Prone stretch** - lay on the ground with your back to the floor. Exhale as you straighten your arms and legs. Your fingers and toes should be stretching in opposite directions. Hold this stretch for thirty seconds.
- **Groin stretch** - sit on the ground with the soles of your feet touching each other. Grab hold of your feet and slowly pull yourself forward until mild tension is felt in your groin region. Hold this position for a minimum of sixty seconds.

Avoiding Overtraining & Burnout

Burnout is defined as a negative emotional state acquired by physical overtraining. Some symptoms of burnout include physical illness, boredom, anxiety, disinterest in training, and general sluggish behavior. Whether you are a beginner or expert, you're susceptible to burnout. Here are a few suggestions to help avoid burnout in your training:

1. Make your workouts intense but enjoyable.
2. Vary your training routine (i.e., hard day/easy day routine).
3. Train to different types of music.
4. Pace yourself during your workouts - don't try to do it all in one day.
5. Listen to your body- if you don't feel up to training, skip a day. Missing a day or two won't kill you.
6. Work out in different types of environments.
7. Use different types of training equipment.
8. Work out with different training partners.

9. Keep accurate records of your training routine.
10. Vary the intensity of your training throughout your workout.

What's Next?

Now that we covered the preliminary stuff, it's time to move on to the actual heavy bag routines. So, if you're ready, let's move on to the next chapter.

Heavy Bag Bible

Book Three: Heavy Bag Workout

THE WORKOUT ROUTINES

The Three Training Methodologies

Before introducing you to the heavy bag routines featured in this chapter, it's important to first discuss the three training methodologies.

Essentially, all of the heavy bag routines presented in this book will fall under one of three different types of training methods; they are proficiency training, conditioning training, and street training. Let's take a look at each one.

Conditioning Training

Conditioning Training focuses exclusively on "time-based" workouts and it's primarily used by boxers, mixed martial artists, kickboxers, self-defense technicians, and fitness enthusiasts who wish to train on the heavy bag for specified period of time called *rounds*. Depending on the practitioner's level of conditioning, each round can range anywhere from one to five minutes. Each round is then separated by either 30-second, one-minute or two-minute breaks. A good heavy bag workout consists of at least five to eight rounds.

Conditioning Training is performed at a moderate pace, and it develops cardiovascular fitness, muscular endurance, fluidity, rhythm, distancing, timing, speed, footwork, and balance. Many fitness

Conditioning training can also be used when sparring, shadow boxing, skipping rope, and focus mitt training.

enthusiasts who are looking to burn fat will use this methodology as it tends to burn a significant amount of calories.

Conditioning Training does require that you have a fundamental understanding of combining punches and kicks together into logical combinations.

As I discussed in *Volume 2* of this book series (*Heavy Bag Combinations: The Ultimate Guide to Heavy Bag Punching Combinations*), a combination or *compound attack* is the logical sequence of two or more techniques thrown in strategic succession. For example, a jab followed by a rear cross is considered to be a basic punching combination.

Proficiency Training

The second training methodology is Proficiency Training and it's generally used by martial artists and self-defense practitioners who want to sharpen one specific punch, kick, or strike at a time by executing it over and over for a prescribed number of repetitions. Each time the technique is performed with "clean" form at various speeds. Punches are also carried out with the eyes closed to develop a kinesthetic "feel" for the action.

Proficiency Training on the heavy bag develops speed, power, accuracy, non-telegraphic movement, balance, and psychomotor skill.

Proficiency training is not just limited to martial arts and self-defense. It can also been used by boxers who want to develop and sharpen a specific punching technique. For example, a boxing coach might have his student jab at the bag for a specific amount of repetitions.

Heavy Bag Bible

Street Training

The third and final training methodology is Street Training, and it's specially designed for reality-based self-defense preparation.

Since most self-defense altercations are explosive, lasting an average of 20 seconds, the practitioner must prepare for this possible scenario. This means delivering explosive and powerful compound attacks with vicious intent for approximately 20 seconds, resting one minute, and then repeating the process. Well-conditioned athletes can go longer. In fact, a few of my students are capable of performing the street training methodology uninterrupted for a full minute.

Street Training prepares you for the stress and immediate fatigue of a real fight. It also develops speed, power, explosiveness, target selection and recognition, timing, footwork, pacing, and breath control. You can also practice this methodology in different lighting, on different terrains, and in various environmental settings.

Street Training is not just limited to heavy bag training. For example, you can prepare yourself for multiple assailants by having your training partners attack you with focus mitts from a variety of angles, ranges, and target postures. For 20 seconds, go after them with vicious and powerful offensive techniques.

Street training is predicated on explosiveness. The offensive techniques that barrage the bag should possess a sudden and immediate outburst of violent energy. Your attack should never be progressive in nature; it does not build in speed and power. It begins and ends explosively.

Technique Always Comes First!

Take your time when working out on the heavy bag. If you are learning how to use it for the very first time, I strongly urge you to take your time and develop the proper punching mechanics before tearing into the bag.

Remember, the heavy bag is a serious piece of training equipment, and it is easy to get injured when using it. Heavy bag workouts are also tough and very demanding on the body. Avoid premature exhaustion by pacing yourself during your workouts. Remember, it's not a race! Enjoy the process of learning how to use the bag with skill and finesse.

Again, before you begin any of the exercise programs included in this book, it's important to check with your doctor to see if you have any condition that might be aggravated by strenuous exercise.

Finally, it's time to take a look at the different types of heavy bag workouts. I'll start with the conventional methods first and then work our way to the most obscure methods of heavy bag training.

Workout Routine #1
Time-Based Training

A time-based heavy bag workout is based on rounds, and it's an ideal way to structure your workouts. Before you begin, decide on the duration of your rounds as well as the rest intervals.

In most cases, mixed martial artists, boxers and kick boxers will work the heavy bag for three-minute rounds with one-minute rest periods. Depending on their level of conditioning and specific training goals, they might do this for a total of 5 to 10 rounds.

Initially, you'll need to experiment with both the round duration and rest intervals to see what works best for you. Remember to start off slow and progressively build up the intensity and length of your workouts. Don't forget to work with the bag and not try to kill it!

To get you started, here are some sample time-based workouts you might want to try. Keep in mind, the Advanced Level workouts are for elite fighters who have a minimum of 5 years of heavy bag training and conditioning.

Besides the actual body mechanics of punching, there are several other elements that comprise a punching combination. They include attack rhythms, height variations, the cadence of delivery, and practitioner movement.

Book Three: Heavy Bag Workout

Sample Time-Based Heavy Bag Workouts

Skill Level	Duration of Each Round	Rest Period	Total Number of rounds
Beginner	1 minute	2 minutes	3
Beginner	1 minute	1 minute	3
Beginner	2 minutes	2 minutes	3
Beginner	2 minutes	1 minute	3
Intermediate	3 minutes	2 minutes	5
Intermediate	3 minutes	1 minute	5
Intermediate	3 minutes	2 minutes	6
Intermediate	3 minutes	1 minute	6
Advanced	4 minutes	2 minutes	8
Advanced	4 minutes	1 minute	8
Advanced	5 minutes	2 minutes	10
Advanced	5 minutes	1 minute	10

All time-based workouts will require you to invest in a workout timer. Luckily, there are dozens of smartphone apps that mimic the same features of an actual interval timer. These workout apps are convenient, inexpensive and can be found at your favorite online app store.

What Combinations Should I Throw?

What follows are just a few punching combinations you can perform during your time-based workouts. If you require advanced heavy bag combination training, including step-by-step photographs, please see *Volume 2* of this book series, *Heavy Bag Combinations: The Ultimate Guide to Heavy Bag Punching Combinations*.

Once again, this book assumes you can perform the basic punching skills, including the jab, rear cross, hook, and uppercut. However, if you are not familiar with these foundational techniques, please see the step-by-step instructions featured in the appendix of this book.

When reading the combination sequence on the following pages, please note the word *high* indicates punches delivered at head level and *low* represents punches delivered to the stomach level on the bag.

Book Three: Heavy Bag Workout

- Jab (high) - Jab (high)
- Jab (low) - Jab (low)
- Jab (high) - Jab (low)
- Jab (low) - Jab (high)
- Jab (high) - Jab (high) - Rear Cross (high)
- Jab (high) - Jab (high) - Rear Cross (low)
- Jab - Rear Cross (high)
- Jab - Rear Cross (low)
- Jab - Rear Cross (high) - Jab
- Jab - Rear Cross (low) - Jab
- Jab - Rear Cross - Jab - Rear Cross
- Jab - Jab - Rear Cross
- Jab - Rear Cross - Jab
- Jab - Rear Cross - Lead Hook (high)
- Jab - Rear Cross - Lead Hook (low)
- Jab - Rear Cross - Lead Hook (high) - Rear Hook (high)
- Jab - Rear Cross - Lead Hook (low) - Rear Hook (low)
- Jab - Rear Cross - Lead Hook (high) - Rear Hook (low)
- Jab - Rear Cross - Lead Hook (low) - Rear Hook (high)
- Jab - Rear Hook (high)
- Jab - Rear Hook (low)

Heavy Bag Bible

- Jab - Lead Hook (high)
- Jab - Lead Hook (low)
- Jab - Lead Hook (high) - Rear hook (high)
- Jab - Lead Hook (low) - Rear hook (low)
- Jab - Lead Hook (high) - Rear hook (low)
- Jab - Lead Hook (low) - Rear hook (high)
- Jab - Jab - Rear Cross - Lead Hook (high)
- Jab - Jab - Rear Cross - Lead Hook (low)
- Jab - Rear Cross - Lead Hook (high) - Rear Uppercut
- Jab - Rear Cross - Lead Hook (high) - Rear Hook (low) - Lead Uppercut
- Rear Cross - Lead Hook - Lead Hook - Rear Hook (low-high-high-low)
- Rear Cross - Lead Hook - Lead Hook - Rear Hook (high-low-low-high)
- Rear Cross - Lead Hook - Rear Cross - Lead Hook - Rear Hook (high-high-low-high-low)
- Rear Uppercut - Lead Hook (high)
- Rear Uppercut - Lead Hook (low)
- Rear Uppercut - Lead Hook (high) - Rear Hook (high)
- Rear Uppercut - Lead Hook (low) - Rear Hook (low)
- Rear Uppercut - Lead Hook (high) - Rear Hook (low)

Book Three: Heavy Bag Workout

Workout Routine #2
Ambidextrous Training

Ambidexterity is the ability to perform with equal facility on both the right and left sides of the body. In simpler terms, it's the capacity to use the right and left hands equally well.

Ambidexterity is a vital attribute for reality-based self-defense training. In fact, it's a regular part of my teaching curriculum. Here are three important reasons why: (1) your strong or dominant hand might be injured in combat, (2) you might be assaulted on the weak side of your body, and (3) your strong hand might be occupied (i.e., holding or carrying an object) during the moment of the assault.

When it comes to high-risk self-defense training, ambidexterity must also be mastered in the following components of combat.

Heavy Bag Bible

1. Stances -both armed and unarmed combat stances.
2. Submission Holds - including the vertical and horizontal grappling planes.
3. Natural Body Weapons - kicks, punches, and various other striking techniques.
4. Natural Defensive Techniques - blocks, parries, and evasion movements.
5. Knives Fighting
6. Stick Fighting
7. Makeshift Weapons
8. Chemical Irritants
9. Firearm Skills

Ambidexterity for Boxing and Mixed Martial Arts

Ambidexterity is also an invaluable skill for combat sports like boxing, kickboxing, and mixed martial arts. In fact, the ability to fight your opponent from both right (southpaw) and left (orthodox) stances can be advantageous for some of the following reasons.

1. **Opens the opponent up** - Since most boxers are right-handed, they are used to fighting against other right-handed fighters. However, switching from an orthodox to a southpaw stance opens your opponent up to several angular attacks.
2. **Lead hand power & accuracy** - Assuming you are right-handed, switching to a southpaw stance places your most accurate and coordinated hand closer to the opponent. This allows you to jab with greater power and accuracy.
3. **Weak hand power enhancer** - A southpaw stance also brings your weaker left hand back to the rear side of your body. This means greater impact power when delivering rear punches

(i.e., rear cross, hook, and uppercut).

4. **It confuses your opponent** - Finally, switching from an orthodox to a southpaw stance (in the middle if a fight) will undoubtedly confuse the hell out of your opponent and throw off his timing and footwork. In most cases, it will take a couple rounds for him to get his bearing straight. This creates an enormous window of opportunity that you can exploit to your advantage.

Ambidexterity and Heavy Bag Training

There are numerous ways you can incorporate ambidexterity training to your heavy bag workouts. Here are just a few.

1. **Switch after every round** - Begin your first round on the heavy bag from an orthodox (left lead) stance and deliver all of your punching combinations from this position. During the next round, switch to a southpaw (right lead) stance and deliver all of your combinations from this posture. Every round, switch between right and left stances for a total of 8 to 10 rounds.

2. **Switch after every combination** - Deliver a specific combination (i.e., jab-rear cross-lead hook-rear hook) from an orthodox stance. Next, switch to a southpaw stance and perform the same heavy bag combination. Switch back to the orthodox stance and perform another combination. Once again, change to a southpaw stance and deliver the same combination on the bag. Go back and forth between stances for the duration of your round. Perform this for a total of 8 to 10 rounds.

3. **Switch after circling** - From an orthodox stance, deliver a series of combinations while rotating 360-degrees around the bag. Once your circle is complete, switch to a southpaw stance and execute a series of combinations while circling the opposite direction around the bag. Switch back and forth between right and left stances for a total of 8 to 10 rounds.

While many boxing purists will argue against switching stances, there are others who disagree. For example, professional boxers like Marvin Hagler, Michael Moorer, Roy Jones Jr., Manny Pacquiao, and Erik Morales are known for switching their stances during a match.

Ambidextrous Training
Switching Your Stance After Every Round

Round	Stance	Round Duration	Rest Period
1	orthodox	3 minutes	1 minute
2	southpaw	3 minutes	1 minute
3	orthodox	3 minutes	1 minute
4	southpaw	3 minutes	1 minute
5	orthodox	3 minutes	1 minute
6	southpaw	3 minutes	1 minute
7	orthodox	3 minutes	1 minute
8	southpaw	3 minutes	1 minute
9	orthodox	3 minutes	1 minute
10	southpaw	3 minutes	1 minute

Some boxing coaches and trainers will argue that it's too difficult for a fighter to maintain two stances. However, I categorically disagree! As a matter of fact, I've maintained fighting proficiency with both the right and left stances for over 30 years. The bottom line is, if you want something bad enough, you can make it happen!

Heavy Bag Bible

Switching After Every Combination

Stance	Combination Sequence
orthodox	Jab (high) - Jab (high)
southpaw	Jab (high) - Jab (high)
orthodox	Jab (high) - Jab (low)
southpaw	Jab (high) - Jab (low)
orthodox	Jab (high) - Jab (high) - Rear Cross (low)
southpaw	Jab (high) - Jab (high) - Rear Cross (low)
orthodox	Jab - Rear Cross - Lead Hook (high)
southpaw	Jab - Rear Cross - Lead Hook (high)
orthodox	Jab - Rear Cross - Lead Hook (low) - Rear Hook (low)
southpaw	Jab - Rear Cross - Lead Hook (low) - Rear Hook (low)
orthodox	Jab - Lead Hook (low) - Rear hook (low)
southpaw	Jab - Lead Hook (low) - Rear hook (low)
orthodox	Jab - Jab - Rear Cross - Lead Hook (high)
southpaw	Jab - Jab - Rear Cross - Lead Hook (high)
orthodox	Rear Cross - Lead Hook - Lead Hook - Rear Hook (all high)
southpaw	Rear Cross - Lead Hook - Lead Hook - Rear Hook (all high)

Switching After Circling

Stance	Combination Sequence	Direction of Movement
orthodox	Jab (high) - Jab (high)	Circle left
southpaw	Jab (high) - Jab (high)	Circle right
orthodox	Jab (high) - Jab (low)	Circle left
southpaw	Jab (high) - Jab (low)	Circle right
orthodox	Jab (high) - Jab (high) - Rear Cross (low)	Circle left
southpaw	Jab (high) - Jab (high) - Rear Cross (low)	Circle right
orthodox	Jab - Rear Cross - Lead Hook (high)	Circle left
southpaw	Jab - Rear Cross - Lead Hook (high)	Circle right
orthodox	Jab - Rear Cross - Lead Hook (low) - Rear Hook (low)	Circle left
southpaw	Jab - Rear Cross - Lead Hook (low) - Rear Hook (low)	Circle right
orthodox	Jab - Lead Hook (low) - Rear hook (low)	Circle left
southpaw	Jab - Lead Hook (low) - Rear hook (low)	Circle right
orthodox	Jab - Jab - Rear Cross - Lead Hook (high)	Circle left
southpaw	Jab - Jab - Rear Cross - Lead Hook (high)	Circle right
orthodox	Rear Cross - Lead Hook - Lead Hook - Rear Hook (all high)	Circle left
southpaw	Rear Cross - Lead Hook - Lead Hook - Rear Hook (all high)	Circle right

Workout Routine #3
Elevation Drill

The elevation drill is one of the most demanding exercises you can perform on the heavy bag. Besides requiring a tremendous amount of muscular endurance, the drill also requires a significant amount of mental resilience and attention control.

The objective of this exercise is to keep the heavy bag elevated at a 45-degree angle by continuously punching it. This drill is brutal on the arms. In fact, the average person can barely last 30 seconds. To perform the drill follow these steps:

1. Face the heavy bag and assume a fighting stance.
2. Deliver the jab and rear cross combination continuously. Concentrate on delivering full-speed, full-force punches.
3. Maintain a rapid-fire cadence to keep the bag elevated at a

Book Three: Heavy Bag Workout

45-degree angle from the floor.

4. Avoid pushing the bag and remember to snap each blow. If the heavy bag spins when performing this exercise, it means your punches are not landing at the center of the bag. Remember to focus your blows at a single target point.

5. Perform the drill for a minimum of three rounds. Each round can last anywhere from 10 to 90 seconds. If you are exceptionally conditioned, go for 90 seconds.

The goal of the elevation drill is to keep the heavy bag elevated at approximately 45-degrees by continuously punching it.

Be very careful when performing this exercise. One misplaced punch or bent wrist can easily lead to a severe injury.

363

Heavy Bag Bible

Elevation Drill Demonstration

Step 1: The practitioner assumes a fighting stance.

Step 2: He begins with a powerful jab.

Book Three: Heavy Bag Workout

Step 3: He immediately follows with a rear cross.

Step 4: Next, another powerful jab.

Heavy Bag Bible

Step 5: The speed and power of the blows elevate the heavy bag at a 45-degree angle.

Step 6: To keep the bag elevated at 45-degrees, the practitioner must continue to attack the heavy bag with vicious intent.

Book Three: Heavy Bag Workout

Step 7: The practitioner delivers another rapid-fire rear across.

Step 8: Followed by another powerful jab.

Heavy Bag Bible

Step 9: The practitioner continues his barrage for a total of 60 seconds.

While the elevation drill is designed to be a self-standing workout routine, some boxers will only perform this exercise during the last 10 seconds of a 3 minute heavy bag round.

Elevation Drill Workout Routines

Skill Level	Duration of Each Round	Rest Period	Total Number of rounds
Beginner	10 seconds	2 minutes	3
Beginner	15 seconds	1 minute	3
Beginner	20 seconds	2 minutes	3
Beginner	25 minutes	1 minute	3
Intermediate	30 seconds	2 minutes	5
Intermediate	35 seconds	1 minute	5
Intermediate	40 seconds	2 minutes	5
Intermediate	45 seconds	1 minute	5
Advanced	60 seconds	2 minutes	6
Advanced	70 seconds	1 minute	6
Advanced	80 seconds	2 minutes	6
Advanced	90 seconds	1 minute	6

Workout Routine #4
Piston Punching

Piston Punching is another demanding heavy bag exercise that will push you to your limits. Your objective is to fire off linear blows in a rapid-fire or piston-like fashion *without elevating the bag*. Piston punching can be directed to both high and low heavy bag targets.

Like the elevation drill, this exercise is very taxing on the shoulders, so remember to take your time and gradually increase the intensity of this exercise. To perform piston punching, follow these steps:

1. Face the heavy bag and assume a fighting stance.
2. Deliver the jab and rear cross combination continuously. Concentrate on delivering full-speed, full-force punches.
3. Focus on snapping each punch and *avoid* elevating the bag.

Book Three: Heavy Bag Workout

4. If the bag spins when performing this exercise, it means your punches are not landing at the center. Remember to focus all of your blows to a single center point on the bag.
5. Perform the drill for a minimum of three rounds. Each round can last anywhere from 10 to 60 seconds. If you are exceptionally conditioned, go for 90 seconds.

The following photographs demonstrate piston punching at high targets on the heavy bag. Keep in mind that all of these pictures were taken in real-time speed.

Piston Punching Demonstration (high targets only)

Step 1: The drill begins with a powerful jab at the bag.

Heavy Bag Bible

Step 2: Followed by a rear cross.

Step 3: Next, another powerful jab.

Book Three: Heavy Bag Workout

Step 4: The author continues with another rear cross at the bag.

Step 5: He follows up with another jab.

373

Heavy Bag Bible

Step 6: Next, another rear cross. Notice how all of his punches are delivered at the center of the bag.

Step 8: Mr. Franco continues his assault for a total of 30 seconds.

Book Three: Heavy Bag Workout

Piston Punching Workout Routines

Skill Level	Duration of Each Round	Rest Period	Total Number of rounds
Beginner	10 seconds	2 minutes	3
Beginner	15 seconds	1 minute	3
Beginner	20 seconds	2 minutes	3
Beginner	25 minutes	1 minute	3
Intermediate	30 seconds	2 minutes	5
Intermediate	35 seconds	1 minute	5
Intermediate	40 seconds	2 minutes	5
Intermediate	45 seconds	1 minute	5
Advanced	60 seconds	2 minutes	6
Advanced	70 seconds	1 minute	6
Advanced	80 seconds	2 minutes	6
Advanced	90 seconds	1 minute	6

Workout Routine #5
Cyclone Drill

The Cyclone Drill develops bone-crushing hook punches. The objective of the exercise is to assault the heavy bag with a continuous flurry of hook punches delivered in a back and forth fashion. Like piston punching, this drill permits you to strike both high and low heavy bag targets. To perform the Cyclone drill, follow these steps:

1. Face the heavy bag and assume a fighting stance.
2. Deliver the lead and rear hook punches in a fluid, back and forth fashion. Concentrate on striking the bag as fast and hard as possible.
3. Perform the drill for a minimum of three rounds. Each round can last anywhere from 10 to 90 seconds.

Book Three: Heavy Bag Workout

Cyclone Drill Demonstration

Step 1: The practitioner throws a high lead hook punch at the bag.

Step 2: Next, a rear hook.

377

Heavy Bag Bible

Step 3: Followed by a lead hook.

Step 4: He continues with a rear hook.

Book Three: Heavy Bag Workout

Step 5: Then another high lead hook punch.

Step 6: The practitioner continues his assault for a total of 30 seconds.

Cyclone Drill Workout Routines

Skill Level	Duration of Each Round	Rest Period	Total Number of rounds
Beginner	10 seconds	2 minutes	3
Beginner	15 seconds	1 minute	3
Beginner	20 seconds	2 minutes	3
Beginner	25 minutes	1 minute	3
Intermediate	30 seconds	2 minutes	5
Intermediate	35 seconds	1 minute	5
Intermediate	40 seconds	2 minutes	5
Intermediate	45 seconds	1 minute	5
Advanced	60 seconds	2 minutes	6
Advanced	70 seconds	1 minute	6
Advanced	80 seconds	2 minutes	6
Advanced	90 seconds	1 minute	6

Book Three: Heavy Bag Workout

Workout Routine #6
"Hit the Seam" Drill

I developed this unusual exercise approximately 25 years ago. My goal was to design a heavy bag drill that would improve both punching power and accuracy at the same time. As you might already know, the heavy bag is primarily designed for striking power, not target accuracy. However, this drill allows you to simultaneously develop both striking power and target accuracy.

The objective of the drill is to deliberately throw punching combinations at the stitching seam that runs vertically down the heavy bag. This is especially challenging because the heavy bag swings and spins uncontrollably. So you will be forced to move continuously with the bag to ensure proper targeting.

"Hit the seam" also develops target recognition along the opponent's centerline. Essentially, target recognition is the ability to immediately recognize strategic anatomical targets during a

Heavy Bag Bible

fight. Depending on what you are training for (i.e., boxing, mixed martial arts, kickboxing, military combatives, street fighting, etc), the opponent's targets might include his eyes, temple, nose, chin, back of neck, throat, solar plexus, ribs, groin, thighs, knees, and shins.

The Centerline

"Hit the seam" is also ideal for teaching you how to strike the opponent's centerline. The centerline is an imaginary vertical line that divides the opponent's body in half. Located on this line are some of his vital impact targets. This includes the eyes, nose, chin, throat, solar plexus, and groin. Striking these centerline targets in a fight will disrupt your opponent's balance, inhibit his mobility and maximize impact damage. However, keep in mind that combat sports like boxing, mixed martial arts, and kickboxing have rules and regulations that will limit which centerline targets you can strike.

The proper placement of your centerline (in relation to your opponent) is also important and will directly effect your target exposure, balance, mobility, and punching power.

"Hit the Seam" Drill Variations

There are three variations of this drill, and they are listing in order of increased difficulty:

1. Hit the Seam - straight punches only
2. Hit the Seam - circular punches only
3. Hit the Seam - all punches

"Hit the Seam" - Straight Punches Only

This is the easiest of all three variations. It requires you to only throw linear combinations (i.e., jab-jab-rear cross-jab) at the heavy bag seam. Since the heavy bag seam runs vertically down the bag, you can throw both high and low straight punches. Some of them might include the following:

- Jab (high) - Jab (high)
- Jab (low) - Jab (low)
- Jab (high) - Jab (low)
- Jab (low) - Jab (high)
- Jab (high) - Jab (high) - Rear Cross (high)
- Jab (high) - Jab (high) - Rear Cross (low)
- Jab - Rear Cross (high)
- Jab - Rear Cross (low)
- Jab - Rear Cross (high) - Jab
- Jab - Rear Cross (low) - Jab
- Jab - Rear Cross - Jab - Rear Cross

Heavy Bag Bible

- Jab - Jab - Rear Cross
- Jab - Rear Cross - Jab

"Hit the Seam" - Circular Punches Only

This drill variation requires an intermediate level of heavy bag skill. The goal is to only throw circular punches (hooks, shovel hooks, and uppercuts) at the stitching seam of the heavy bag. Again, since the stitching runs vertically down the bag, you can throw circular punches at both high and low targets. Punching combinations can include some of the following:

- Lead Hook (high) - Rear Hook (high)
- Lead Hook (low) - Lead Hook (low)
- Lead Hook (high) - Rear Hook (low)
- Lead Hook (low) - Rear Hook (high)
- Lead Hook (high) - Lead Hook (high) - Rear Hook (high)
- Lead Hook (high) - Lead Hook (high) - Rear Hook (low)
- Lead Hook (high) - Rear Uppercut (low)
- Lead Hook (high) - - Rear Hook (high) - Rear Uppercut (low)
- Rear Uppercut (low) - Lead Uppercut (low)
- Rear Uppercut (low) - Lead Uppercut (low) - Lead Hook (high) - Rear Hook (high)
- Rear Uppercut (high) - Lead Uppercut (high) - Lead Hook (low) - Rear Hook (low)

"Hit the Seam" - All Punches

This is by far the most challenging of the three variations. It requires you to throw your entire punching arsenal at the seam line. This includes the jab, rear cross, hook, shovel hook, and uppercut. Once again, your punches can be delivered to both high and low heavy bag targets. Some striking combinations can include:

- Jab - Jab - Rear Uppercut (all high)
- Jab - Lead Uppercut - Rear Cross (all high)
- Jab - Lead Uppercut - Rear Cross (low-high-low)
- Jab - Rear Uppercut - Lead Uppercut (all high)
- Jab - Rear Uppercut - Lead Uppercut - Rear Cross - Lead Hook (all high)
- Jab - Rear Cross - Lead Hook - Rear Uppercut (all high)
- Jab - Rear Cross - Lead Hook - Rear Cross (all high)
- Jab - rear cross - Lead Hook - Rear Cross - Lead Hook - Lead Hook (5x high -1 low)
- Rear Cross - Jab - Rear Hook (all high)
- Rear Cross - Jab - Rear Hook - Lead Uppercut - Lead Hook (high-high-low-high-high)
- Rear Cross - Lead Hook - Rear Cross - Lead Hook - Rear Uppercut (high-high-high-low-high)
- Rear Hook - Lead Hook - Rear Hook - Lead Uppercut (all high)

Heavy Bag Bible

Since the heavy bag seam runs vertically down the bag, you can throw both high and low punching combinations.

"Hit the Seam" Workout Routines

Skill Level	Duration of Each Round	Rest Period	Total Number of rounds
Beginner	1 minute	2 minutes	3
Beginner	1 minute	1 minute	3
Beginner	2 minutes	2 minutes	3
Beginner	2 minutes	1 minute	3
Intermediate	3 minutes	2 minutes	5
Intermediate	3 minutes	1 minute	5
Intermediate	3 minutes	2 minutes	6
Intermediate	3 minutes	1 minute	6
Advanced	4 minutes	2 minutes	8
Advanced	4 minutes	1 minute	8
Advanced	5 minutes	2 minutes	10
Advanced	5 minutes	1 minute	10

If you want to really push yourself, you can combine different routines into a single workout. For example, try combining ambidextrous training with "hit the seam" drill.

Workout Routine #7
X-Training

X-Training is also another methodology that improves both punching power and target accuracy. Compared the previous drill, X-Training is less restrictive. The objective of the exercise is to throw punching combinations at Xs that are on the heavy bag.

Preparing the Bag

The best way to prepare your heavy bag for X-Training is first to cut several small pieces of white electrical tape into two-inch strips. Next, cross two pieces of tape and form an X and press it firmly into the heavy bag. Space the Xs approximately six inches apart from each other and distribute them around the bag. Make certain to place both high and low targets on the bag (see photo).

X-Training Variations

There are three variations of X-Training, and they are listing in order of increased difficulty:

1. X-Training - straight punches only
2. X-Training - circular punches only
3. X-Training - all punches

X-Training works best on leather and vinyl covered heavy bags. Unfortunately, electrical tape won't stick to canvas bags.

Book Three: Heavy Bag Workout

Pictured here, a heavy bag prepped for X-Training.

Heavy Bag Bible

X-Training - Straight Punches Only

This is the easiest of all three variations. It requires you to only throw linear combinations (i.e., jab-jab-rear cross-jab) at the Xs. Some of them might include the following:

- Jab (high) - Jab (high)
- Jab (low) - Jab (low)
- Jab (high) - Jab (low)
- Jab (low) - Jab (high)
- Jab (high) - Jab (high) - Rear Cross (high)
- Jab (high) - Jab (high) - Rear Cross (low)
- Jab - Rear Cross (high)
- Jab - Rear Cross (low)
- Jab - Rear Cross (high) - Jab
- Jab - Rear Cross (low) - Jab
- Jab - Rear Cross - Jab - Rear Cross
- Jab - Jab - Rear Cross
- Jab - Rear Cross - Jab

X-Training - Circular Punches Only

This drill variation requires an intermediate level of heavy bag skill. The goal is to only throw circular punches (hooks, shovel hooks, and uppercuts) at the white targets. Punching combinations can include some of the following:

- Lead Hook (high) - Rear Hook (high)
- Lead Hook (low) - Lead Hook (low)
- Lead Hook (high) - Rear Hook (low)
- Lead Hook (low) -Rear Hook (high)
- Lead Hook (high) - Lead Hook (high) - Rear Hook (high)
- Lead Hook (high) - Lead Hook (high) - Rear Hook (low)
- Lead Hook (high) - Rear Uppercut (low)
- Lead Hook (high) - - Rear Hook (high) - Rear Uppercut (low)
- Rear Uppercut (low) - Lead Uppercut (low)
- Rear Uppercut (low) - Lead Uppercut (low) - Lead Hook (high) - Rear Hook (high)
- Rear Uppercut (high) - Lead Uppercut (high) - Lead Hook (low) - Rear Hook (low)

X-Training - All Punches

This is the most challenging of the three variations. It requires you to throw your entire punching arsenal at the Xs. This includes the jab, rear cross, hook, shovel hook, and uppercut. Once again, your punches can be delivered to both high and low heavy bag targets. Some striking combinations can include:

- Jab - Jab- Rear Uppercut (all high)
- Jab - Lead Uppercut - Rear Cross (all high)
- Jab - Lead Uppercut - Rear Cross (low-high-low)
- Jab - Rear Uppercut - Lead Uppercut (all high)

Heavy Bag Bible

- Jab - Rear Uppercut - Lead Uppercut - Rear Cross - Lead Hook (all high)
- Jab - Rear Cross - Lead Hook - Rear Uppercut (all high)
- Jab - Rear Cross - Lead Hook - Rear Cross (all high)
- Jab - rear cross - Lead Hook - Rear Cross - Lead Hook - Lead Hook (5x high -1 low)
- Rear Cross - Jab - Rear Hook (all high)
- Rear Cross - Jab - Rear Hook - Lead Uppercut - Lead Hook (high-high-low-high-high)
- Rear Cross - Lead Hook - Rear Cross - Lead Hook - Rear Uppercut (high-high-high-low-high)
- Rear Hook - Lead Hook - Rear Hook - Lead Uppercut (all high)

If you are training for a competitive match, always workout on the bag with a mouthpiece in your mouth. Remember, train the way you will fight and fight the way you train!

Book Three: Heavy Bag Workout

X-Training Workout Routines

Skill Level	Duration of Each Round	Rest Period	Total Number of rounds
Beginner	1 minute	2 minutes	3
Beginner	1 minute	1 minute	3
Beginner	2 minutes	2 minutes	3
Beginner	2 minutes	1 minute	3
Intermediate	3 minutes	2 minutes	5
Intermediate	3 minutes	1 minute	5
Intermediate	3 minutes	2 minutes	6
Intermediate	3 minutes	1 minute	6
Advanced	4 minutes	2 minutes	8
Advanced	4 minutes	1 minute	8
Advanced	5 minutes	2 minutes	10
Advanced	5 minutes	1 minute	10

Learn to relax and avoid tensing your muscles when throwing combinations. Muscular tension will throw off your timing, retard the speed of your punches, and wear you out during a round.

Workout Routine #8
"Punch-a Hole" Exercise

Any boxer worth his salt will tell you that heavy bag training is a delicate mixture of power, speed, timing, and pacing. However, the real secret to making it through a full three-minute round on the heavy bag is to pace the power of your strikes.

Some of you might already know that full force, full speed punching will invariably lead to a very short-lived training round. In most instances, the average person can only sustain "all out" power punching for approximately 30 seconds. That's also assuming they are punching with proper form.

The "Punch a Hole" exercise goes against this conventional wisdom by training you to hit the bag as hard as humanly possible. In essence, your goal is to literally try and punch a hole through the heavy bag. Is this actually possible? I seriously doubt it! Nevertheless, this type of training will transform your fists into sledgehammers.

Book Three: Heavy Bag Workout

"Punch a Hole" Workout Demonstration

Step 1: The practitioner assumes a fighting stance.

Step 2: He throws a rear cross punch.

Heavy Bag Bible

Step 3: Next, he follows up with a strong jab.

Step 4: He drives a powerful low rear uppercut.

Book Three: Heavy Bag Workout

Step 5: A high lead hook punch.

Step 6: Followed by a bone-shattering rear cross.

Heavy Bag Bible

Step 7: Another explosive jab.

Step 8: The practitioner continues his assault for a total of 30 seconds.

Book Three: Heavy Bag Workout

Beginner Level
"Punch a Hole" Workout Routines

Workout Routine	Duration of Each Round	Rest Period	Total Number of rounds
1	10 seconds	2 minutes	3
2	10 seconds	1 minute	3
3	15 seconds	2 minutes	3
4	15 seconds	1 minute	3
5	20 seconds	2 minutes	3
6	20 seconds	1 minute	3
7	25 seconds	2 minutes	3
8	25 seconds	1 minute	3
9	10 seconds	1 minute	5
10	15 seconds	2 minutes	5
11	20 seconds	1 minute	5
12	25 seconds	2 minutes	5

The "punch a hole" drill requires you to hit the bag as hard as possible! Do not perform this exercise unless you are absolutely certain you have mastered the proper body mechanics of punching.

Heavy Bag Bible

Intermediate Level
"Punch a Hole" Workout Routines

Workout Routine	Duration of Each Round	Rest Period	Total Number of rounds
1	30 seconds	2 minutes	3
2	30 seconds	1 minute	3
3	35 seconds	2 minutes	3
4	35 seconds	1 minute	3
5	40 seconds	2 minutes	3
6	40 seconds	1 minute	3
7	45 seconds	2 minutes	3
8	45 seconds	1 minute	3
9	30 seconds	1 minute	5
10	35 seconds	2 minutes	5
11	40 seconds	1 minute	5
12	45 seconds	2 minutes	5

Performing this drill for a duration of 30-45 seconds might not seem like a lot. However, I can assure you that after 5 rounds you will be thoroughly exhausted.

Book Three: Heavy Bag Workout

Advanced Level
"Punch a Hole" Workout Routines

Workout Routine	Duration of Each Round	Rest Period	Total Number of rounds
1	50 seconds	2 minutes	4
2	50 seconds	1 minute	4
3	55 seconds	2 minutes	4
4	55 seconds	1 minute	4
5	60 seconds	2 minutes	5
6	60 seconds	1 minute	5
7	65 seconds	2 minutes	5
8	65 seconds	1 minute	5
9	50 seconds	1 minute	6
10	55 seconds	2 minutes	6
11	60 seconds	1 minute	6
12	65 seconds	2 minutes	6

Performing this drill for a duration of 60 seconds or longer is generally reserved for professional fighters who want peak combat performance.

Workout Routine #9
Technique Isolation Training

Technique Isolation training is a variation of my proficiency training methodology. The purpose of this exercise is to focus exclusively on one punch (i.e., jab, rear cross, lead hook, etc.) for your entire workout. For example, if you wanted to sharpen and develop your jab, you would isolate and practice it exclusively on the heavy bag for a specified number of rounds.

> *"I fear not the man who has practiced 10,000 kicks once, but I fear the man who has practiced one kick 10,000 times."*
>
> -Bruce Lee

Book Three: Heavy Bag Workout

Isolation Training (Jab) Demonstration

Step 1: The practitioner assumes a stance.

Step 2: He delivers a high left jab.

403

Heavy Bag Bible

Step 3: He begins circling the bag in a clockwise direction.

Step 4: He throws a low jab

Book Three: Heavy Bag Workout

Step 5: As he moves around the bag, he throws another high jab.

Step 6: Next, another low jab.

405

Heavy Bag Bible

Step 7: Followed by a high jab.

Step 8: He delivers another low jab and continues to circle around the heavy

Book Three: Heavy Bag Workout

Step 9: He fires off another high jab.

Step 10: The practitioner continues jabbing and moving around the at the bag for a duration of 3 minutes.

Technique Isolation Workout Routines

Skill Level	Duration of Each Round	Rest Period	Total Number of rounds
Beginner	1 minute	2 minutes	3
Beginner	1 minute	1 minute	3
Beginner	2 minutes	2 minutes	3
Beginner	2 minutes	1 minute	3
Intermediate	3 minutes	2 minutes	5
Intermediate	3 minutes	1 minute	5
Intermediate	3 minutes	2 minutes	6
Intermediate	3 minutes	1 minute	6
Advanced	4 minutes	2 minutes	8
Advanced	4 minutes	1 minute	8
Advanced	5 minutes	2 minutes	10
Advanced	5 minutes	1 minute	10

In order to maximize the full benefit of technique isolation training, it's important to stick to only one punch for your entire workout. For example, if you're a beginner who wants to perfect your jab, you would practice it exclusively for a total of 3 rounds.

Book Three: Heavy Bag Workout

Workout Routine #10
Defensive Bag Training

Heavy bag training isn't just about offense. In fact, there are several drills designed to sharpen your defensive techniques and improve your defensive reaction time.

A good defensive structure requires mastery of the following four tools: blocks, parries, slipping, and footwork. I can say without reservation that all of these defensive techniques work effectively against boxers, street brawlers, and martial artists of all styles and backgrounds. However, before I can discuss the specific defensive tools, it's important to talk about defensive reaction time when fighting.

What is Defensive Reaction Time?

Defensive reaction time is defined as the elapsed time between the opponent's attack (e.g., jab, hook, rear cross) and your defensive

Heavy Bag Bible

response to that attack (e.g., block, parry, evasion movement). Your defensive reaction time is the result of three fluid stages (defensive recognition, defensive selection, and defensive execution).

1. **Defensive recognition** is the first stage where you recognize and identify that an attack has occurred.
2. **Defensive selection** is the second stage where you immediately select the appropriate defensive tool, technique, or response.
3. **Defensive execution** is the third and final phase where your body performs the appropriate defensive tool, technique, or response.

```
                    DEFENSIVE REACTION
                          TIME
          ┌───────────────┼───────────────┐
  DEFENSIVE RECOGNITION           DEFENSIVE EXECUTION
                          │
                  DEFENSIVE SELECTION
```

Defensive reaction time is the result of three fluid stages: defensive recognition, defensive selection, and defensive execution.

How To Minimize Defensive Reaction Time

When it comes to fighting (including both sport and street), your objective is to minimize your defensive reaction time as much as possible. Luckily, there are several ways to accomplish this.

First, try to be able to read advance information about the opponent's attack. This is referred to as *telegraphic cognizance*. For example, when your opponent chambers his arm back prior to delivering a punch.

Book Three: Heavy Bag Workout

Second, limit your number of defensive responses to a particular type of attack. For example, if your opponent attacks with a jab to your head, you should have only *one specific* defensive response programmed. In this instance, you would parry or deflect the threatening blow.

Third, all of your defensive responses should be natural and performed in a simple fashion. Again, in the case of the jab, not only would you execute a horizontal parry, but you would also situate it on the same side of the opponent's attack (this is called mirror-image parrying).

Fourth, practice, practice, practice! Your defensive responses must be practiced over and over again until they become second nature. Sparring, shadowboxing, focus mitt drills, and even heavy bag training will help you develop these important skills.

Before we get into the defensive heavy bag exercise, let's review all of the different defensive techniques you would use in a fight.

Arm Blocks

Blocks are defensive techniques designed to intercept your assailant's circular attacks. Blocks are executed by placing a non vital body part between the opponent's strike and your body target. There are three primary blocks with which you need to be proficient. They include high blocks, mid-blocks, and elbow blocks.

Never forget that offense is only half the game. Defensive skills are just as important and they must be practiced frequently to ensure that you will survive in the streets as well as the ring.

High Block

The high block is primarily used for street self-defense and it's designed to protect you against overhead blows. To execute the lead high block, simply raise your lead arm up and extend your forearm out and above your head. Be careful not to position your arm where your head is exposed. Make certain that your hand is open and not clenched. This will increase the surface area of your block and provide a quick counterattack. The mechanics for the lead high block are the same as for the rear high block. Raise your rear arm up and extend your forearm out and above your head.

The high block.

Mid-Block

The mid-block is used to defend against circular blows to your head or upper torso. To perform the block, raise either your right or left arm at approximately 90 degrees while simultaneously pronating (rotating) it into the direction of the strike. Make contact with the belly of your forearm at the assailant's wrist or forearm. This movement will provide maximum structural integrity for the blocking tool. Make certain that your hand is held open to increase the surface area of your block.

The mid block.

Elbow Block

The elbow block is frequently used in boxing, kickboxing, and mixed martial arts. It's designed to stop circular blows to your midsection, such as uppercuts, shovel hooks, and even hook kicks. To execute the elbow block, drop your elbow and simultaneously twist your body toward your centerline. Be certain to keep your elbow perpendicular to the floor and keep your hands relaxed and close to your chest. The elbow block can be used on both the right and left sides.

The elbow block.

Hand Parries

The parry is a quick, forceful slap that picks-off and redirects your assailant's linear strike (i.e., jab, and rear cross). There are two general types of parries, horizontal and vertical, and both can be executed with the right and left hands.

Horizontal Parry

To properly execute a horizontal parry from a fighting stance, move your lead hand horizontally across your body (centerline) to deflect and redirect the assailant's punch. Immediately return to your guard position. Be certain to make contact with the palm of your hand. With sufficient training, you can effectively incorporate the horizontal parry into slipping maneuvers.

Pictured here, the horizontal parry.

Vertical Parry

To execute a vertical parry, from a fighting stance, move your hand vertically down your body (centerline) to deflect and redirect the assailant's blow. Once again, don't forget to counterattack your assailant. **CAUTION:** *Do not parry with your fingers. The fingers provide no structural integrity, and they can be jammed or broken easily.*

Slipping

Slipping is a quick defensive maneuver that permits you to avoid an assailant's linear blow (e.g., jab, rear cross) without stepping out of range. Safe and effective slipping requires precise timing and is accomplished by quickly snapping the head and upper torso sideways (right or left) or backward to avoid the oncoming blow. One of the greatest advantages to slipping is that it frees your hands so that you can simultaneously counter your attacker. There are three ways to slip: right, left, and back.

Slipping requires precise timing.

Slipping Right

Begin from a fighting stance and quickly sway your head and upper torso to the right to avoid the assailant's blow. Quickly counterpunch or return to the starting position.

Slipping Left

Start from a fighting stance and quickly sway your head and upper torso to the left to avoid the assailant's linear blow. Quickly counterpunch or return to the starting position.

Slipping Back (or the Snap Back)

Begin from a fighting stance and quickly snap your head back enough to avoid being hit. Quickly counter or return to the starting position.

Footwork

The final component of defense is footwork. In defense, footwork allows you to disengage quickly from the range of attack and quickly re-engage with an effective counterattack.

Footwork facilitates mobility and it's imperative that you constantly move during the course of a fight. Mobility is critical because it makes it difficult for your opponent to hit you, while at the same time enhancing the power of your strikes.

Mobility is defined as your ability to move your body quickly and economically. This can be accomplished through basic footwork. The safest footwork involves quick, economical steps performed on the balls of your feet, while you remain relaxed and balanced.

Basic Footwork Movements

Basic footwork can be used for both offensive and defensive purposes, and it is structured around four general directions: advancing, retreating, sidestepping right, and sidestepping left.

Moving Forward (Advancing)

From your fighting stance, first move your front foot forward (approximately 18 to 24 inches) and then move your rear foot an equal distance.

Moving Backward (Retreating)

From your fighting stance, first move your rear foot backward (approximately 18 to 24 inches) and then move your front foot an equal distance.

Moving Right (Sidestepping Right)

From a fighting stance, first move your right foot to the right (approximately 18 to 24 inches) and then move your left foot an equal distance.

Moving Left (Sidestepping Left)

From a fighting stance, first move your left foot to the left (approximately 18 to 24 inches) and then move your left foot an equal distance.

Practice these four movements every day for 10 to 15 minutes in front of a full-length mirror until your footwork is quick, balanced, and natural.

Book Three: Heavy Bag Workout

The mirror is the best tool for developing quick footwork skills.

Advanced Footwork

Once you have mastered basic footwork, you can incorporate strategic circling into your cache of techniques. Strategic circling is an advanced form of footwork where the fighter uses his lead leg as a pivot point. This advanced footwork can be used defensively to evade an overwhelming assault or offensively to strike the enemy from a strategic angle. Strategic circling can be performed from either a right or left stance.

Circling Right (from a Southpaw Stance)

This means you'll be moving your body around the heavy bag in a counterclockwise direction From a right stance, step 8 to 12 inches to the right with your right foot, then use your right leg as a pivot point and wheel your entire rear leg to the right until the correct stance and positioning is acquired.

Circling Left (from an Orthodox Stance)

This means you'll be moving your body around the heavy bag in a clockwise direction. From a left stance, step 8 to 12 inches to the left with your left foot, then use your left leg as a pivot point and wheel your entire rear leg to the left until the correct stance and positioning is acquired.

Don't forget! You can significantly reduce defensive reaction time by applying some of the following strategies: (1) Recognize advance information about your opponent's attack. (2) Limit your number of defensive options to a particular attack. (3) Make your defensive response natural and simple. (4) Practice, practice, practice!

Sidestep Heavy Bag Drill (with a partner)

Now that we covered all of the defensive techniques it's time to teach you a few defensive oriented heavy bag drills. Let's start with the sidestep drill.

This drill is important for developing evasion skills and for enhancing your sense of range and timing. You'll need a training partner to perform this exercise. To practice the sidestepping drill, employ the following:

1. Face the heavy bag and assume a stance.
2. You training partner holds the heavy bag as you throw punching combinations.
3. At the ideal moment, your training partner forcefully pushes the bag at you.
4. Quickly sidestep away from the bag. If you're standing in a southpaw stance, quickly step with your right foot to the right and move your left leg an equal distance. If you're standing in an orthodox stance, quickly step with your left foot to the left and have your right leg follow an equal distance. When performed correctly, the heavy bag should miss you.
5. Next, your training partner gains control of the swinging bag and you resume throwing combinations.
6. Perform the drill for a minimum of three rounds. Each round can last anywhere from two to five minutes.

Heavy Bag Bible

Holding the Heavy Bag

There are two different ways your training partner can hold the bag for you when performing defensive bag drills.

Pictured here, the close-up holding position.

The extended holding position.

Book Three: Heavy Bag Workout

Skill Level	Duration of Each Round	Rest Period	Total Number of rounds
Beginner	1 minute	2 minutes	3
Beginner	1 minute	1 minute	3
Beginner	2 minutes	2 minutes	3
Beginner	2 minutes	1 minute	3
Intermediate	3 minutes	2 minutes	5
Intermediate	3 minutes	1 minute	5
Intermediate	3 minutes	2 minutes	6
Intermediate	3 minutes	1 minute	6
Advanced	4 minutes	2 minutes	8
Advanced	4 minutes	1 minute	8
Advanced	5 minutes	2 minutes	10
Advanced	5 minutes	1 minute	10

Sidestep Drill Workout Routines (with a partner)

Defensive competency requires you to be adequately prepared to defend against a myriad of adversaries, including poorly skilled opponents. For example, you must be capable of defending against a tight boxer's hook as well as a sloppy, awkward haymaker.

Sidestep Heavy Bag Drill (solo practice)

This is a variation of the sidestep partner drill. Once again, this defensive exercise develops both footwork and timing skills. To perform the exercise, employ the following steps:

1. Face the heavy bag and assume a fighting stance.
2. Begin throwing combinations at the bag.
3. After you complete a few combinations, forcefully push the bag in front of you.
4. When the bags swings back at you, quickly sidestep. If you're standing in a southpaw stance, quickly step with your right foot to the right and have your left leg follow an equal distance. If you're standing in an orthodox stance, quickly step with your left foot to the left and have your right leg follow an equal distance. When performed correctly, the heavy bag should miss you.
5. Reposition yourself and resume throwing combinations at the swinging bag.
6. Perform the drill for a minimum of three rounds. Each round can last anywhere from two to five minutes.

Rope skipping is another effective way of improving your footwork skills. It can be performed as an independent workout or added to your heavy bag routine. Please see the section on interval training for more information.

Sidestep Drill Workout Routines (solo training)

Skill Level	Duration of Each Round	Rest Period	Total Number of rounds
Beginner	1 minute	2 minutes	3
Beginner	1 minute	1 minute	3
Beginner	2 minutes	2 minutes	3
Beginner	2 minutes	1 minute	3
Intermediate	3 minutes	2 minutes	5
Intermediate	3 minutes	1 minute	5
Intermediate	3 minutes	2 minutes	6
Intermediate	3 minutes	1 minute	6
Advanced	4 minutes	2 minutes	8
Advanced	4 minutes	1 minute	8
Advanced	5 minutes	2 minutes	10
Advanced	5 minutes	1 minute	10

A good defensive structure is predicated on a stance that minimizes target exposure, facilitates balance and mobility, and permits quick and evasive movement.

Circling Heavy Bag Drill (with a partner)

This circling drill is another defensive exercise that develops both footwork and counterpunching skills. Once again, you'll need a training partner to perform this exercise. To practice the circling drill, employ the following steps:

1. Face the heavy bag and assume a fighting stance.
2. You training holds the heavy bag while you begin throwing various punching combinations.
3. At the ideal moment, your partner forcefully pushes the bag at you.
4. Quickly circle away from the bag. If you're standing in a southpaw stance, quickly step eight to twelve inches to the right with your right foot, and then use your right leg as a pivot point and wheel your entire rear leg to the right until the correct stance and positioning are acquired. If you're standing in an orthodox stance, quickly step eight to twelve inches to the left with your left foot and then use your left leg as a pivot point and wheel your entire rear leg to the left until the correct stance and positioning are acquired. When performed correctly, the heavy bag should miss you.
5. While simultaneously circling, throw a counterpunch at the swinging bag. The punch you choose will be dependent on a few factors, such as the distance of the target and angle of your body.
6. Perform the drill for a minimum of three rounds. Each round can last anywhere from two to five minutes.

Book Three: Heavy Bag Workout

Circling Drill Workout Routines (with a partner)			
Skill Level	Duration of Each Round	Rest Period	Total Number of rounds
Beginner	1 minute	2 minutes	3
Beginner	1 minute	1 minute	3
Beginner	2 minutes	2 minutes	3
Beginner	2 minutes	1 minute	3
Intermediate	3 minutes	2 minutes	5
Intermediate	3 minutes	1 minute	5
Intermediate	3 minutes	2 minutes	6
Intermediate	3 minutes	1 minute	6
Advanced	4 minutes	2 minutes	8
Advanced	4 minutes	1 minute	8
Advanced	5 minutes	2 minutes	10
Advanced	5 minutes	1 minute	10

When working out on the bag, always be aware of your chin placement. Remember to always keep your chin angled slightly down. This makes you a more elusive target and help minimize direct strikes to your chin and nose. However, avoid forcing your chin down too low. This will inhibit the fluidity of your punches and ultimately slow you down.

427

Circling Heavy Bag Drill (solo practice)

This is a variation of the partner drill. Once again, this defensive exercise develops both footwork and counterpunching skills. To perform the exercise, employ the following steps:

1. Face the heavy bag and assume a fighting stance.
2. Begin throwing combinations at the heavy bag.
3. After a few combinations, push the bag in front of you.
4. When the bag swings back at you, circle away from it. If you're standing in a right (southpaw) stance, quickly step eight to twelve inches to the right with your right foot, and then use your right leg as a pivot point and wheel your entire rear leg to the right until the correct stance and positioning are acquired. If you're standing in a left (orthodox) stance, quickly step eight to twelve inches to the left with your left foot and then use your left leg as a pivot point and wheel your entire rear leg to the left until the correct stance and positioning are acquired. When performed correctly, the heavy bag should miss you.
5. While simultaneously circling, throw a counterpunch at the heavy bag. Again, the punch you choose will be dependent on the distance of the bag and angle of your body.
6. Perform the drill for a minimum of three rounds. Each round can last anywhere from two to five minutes.

Circling Drill Workout Routines (solo training)

Skill Level	Duration of Each Round	Rest Period	Total Number of rounds
Beginner	1 minute	2 minutes	3
Beginner	1 minute	1 minute	3
Beginner	2 minutes	2 minutes	3
Beginner	2 minutes	1 minute	3
Intermediate	3 minutes	2 minutes	5
Intermediate	3 minutes	1 minute	5
Intermediate	3 minutes	2 minutes	6
Intermediate	3 minutes	1 minute	6
Advanced	4 minutes	2 minutes	8
Advanced	4 minutes	1 minute	8
Advanced	5 minutes	2 minutes	10
Advanced	5 minutes	1 minute	10

When moving around the heavy bag, try to maintain a 50-percent weight distribution. This "noncommittal" weight distribution will provide you with the ability to move in any direction quickly and efficiently, while also supplying you with the necessary stability to withstand and defend against various blows.

Slipping Heavy Bag Drill (solo practice)

This is another defensive drill that works on both your slipping and snapback skills. To perform the exercise, employ the following steps:

1. Face the heavy bag and assume a fighting stance.
2. Begin throwing combinations at the bag.
3. After you complete a few combinations, arbitrarily slip your head and body to the side. Try to visualize the opponent's punch coming at you. Remember, it's important that your mental images are clear, strong, and consistent.
4. Return to the stance position and resume punching.
5. Perform the drill for a minimum of three rounds. Each round can last anywhere from two to five minutes.

One of the most important elements of heavy bag training is stability. If stability is compromised, then so is your stance. Here are three principles to keep in mind when trying to achieve stability in your stance: (1) keeping your center of gravity directly over your feet, (2) the lower you drop your center of gravity to its support base, the greater stability you will have, (3) the wider your stance, the greater your stability.

Book Three: Heavy Bag Workout

Slipping Drill Workout Routines (solo training)

Skill Level	Duration of Each Round	Rest Period	Total Number of rounds
Beginner	1 minute	2 minutes	3
Beginner	1 minute	1 minute	3
Beginner	2 minutes	2 minutes	3
Beginner	2 minutes	1 minute	3
Intermediate	3 minutes	2 minutes	5
Intermediate	3 minutes	1 minute	5
Intermediate	3 minutes	2 minutes	6
Intermediate	3 minutes	1 minute	6
Advanced	4 minutes	2 minutes	8
Advanced	4 minutes	1 minute	8
Advanced	5 minutes	2 minutes	10
Advanced	5 minutes	1 minute	10

Slipping can be performed while simultaneously counter punching the opponent. It can also be used in conjunction with parring.

Workout Routine #11
Interval Training

Heavy Bag interval training requires you to alternate between two different activities throughout your workout. For our purposes, we are going to integrate five different activities with the heavy bag. They are:

1. Rope skipping
2. Shadowboxing
3. Double-end bag training
4. Focus mitt training
5. Speed bag training

Rope Skipping Integration

If you want to be quick and light on your feet, you will need to jump rope on a regular basis. Jumping rope is also one of the most effective ways of conditioning your heart and improving coordination, endurance, balance, agility, and body composition.

Fortunately, you can integrate rope skipping into your heavy bag routine. However, one of the most important factors to consider when selecting a rope is the length. A simple method to measure the rope properly is to stand on the center of the rope with one foot. The handles of the rope should reach your armpits.

Interval training with the jump rope requires you to alternate exercises after every round. For example, your first round would include heavy bag training, followed by a round of skipping rope, then heavy bag training, and so on.

What follows are some interval workout routines featuring heavy bag training and rope skipping. For your convenience, I have included beginner, intermediate, and advanced workout programs.

Beginner Level
Interval Workout Routine (Skipping Rope)

Round	Activity	Duration of Each Round	Rest Period
1	Heavy Bag	1 minute	2 minutes
2	Jump Rope	2 minutes	1 minute
3	Heavy Bag	2 minutes	2 minutes
4	Jump Rope	1 minute	1 minute
5	Heavy Bag	2 minutes	2 minutes
6	Jump Rope	2 minutes	1 minute
7	Heavy Bag	1 minute	2 minutes
8	Jump Rope	1 minute	1 minute

Heavy Bag Bible

Intermediate Level
Interval Workout Routine (Skipping Rope)

Round	Activity	Duration of Each Round	Rest Period
1	Heavy Bag	2 minutes	2 minutes
2	Jump Rope	2 minutes	1 minute
3	Heavy Bag	2 minutes	2 minutes
4	Jump Rope	2 minutes	1 minute
5	Heavy Bag	2 minutes	2 minutes
6	Jump Rope	2 minutes	1 minute
7	Heavy Bag	2 minutes	2 minutes
8	Jump Rope	2 minutes	1 minute
9	Heavy Bag	2 minutes	2 minutes
10	Jump Rope	2 minutes	2 minutes

Learning how to skip rope can be very frustrating. Learn to be patient and the skill will come to you. It just takes time!

Book Three: Heavy Bag Workout

Advanced Level
Interval Workout Routine (Skipping Rope)

Round	Activity	Duration of Each Round	Rest Period
1	Heavy Bag	2 minutes	2 minutes
2	Jump Rope	2 minutes	1 minute
3	Heavy Bag	3 minutes	2 minutes
4	Jump Rope	3 minutes	1 minute
5	Heavy Bag	3 minutes	2 minutes
6	Jump Rope	3 minutes	1 minute
7	Heavy Bag	3 minutes	2 minutes
8	Jump Rope	3 minutes	1 minute
9	Heavy Bag	3 minutes	2 minutes
10	Jump Rope	3 minutes	2 minutes
11	Heavy Bag	3 minutes	2 minutes
12	Jump Rope	3 minutes	2 minutes

If you're not careful, you can develop shin splints from skipping rope on hard surfaces like concrete and asphalt. If possible, try to jump rope on a flexible surface like a rubber mat.

Rope Skipping Guidelines

Here are some other guidelines that will help you when skipping rope:

1. Relax your arms and shoulders when jumping.
2. Push off your toes and land gently on the balls of your feet.
3. Use your wrists and forearms to turn the rope, not your shoulders.
4. Maintain good posture and bend naturally at the knees and hips.
5. Jump low, approximately one inch off the ground.
6. Keep your head up and avoid the tendency to look down at your feet.
7. Keep both elbows close to your sides.
8. Avoid jumping rope barefoot.
9. Don't get frustrated by a tangled rope, it's part of the learning process.
10. Jump to different types of music and discover what tunes work best for you.

Shadowboxing Integration

Shadowboxing is the creative deployment of offensive and defensive techniques and maneuvers against an imaginary opponent. It requires intense mental concentration, honest self-analysis, and a deep commitment to improve.

For someone on a tight budget, the good news is that shadowboxing is inexpensive. All you need is a full-length mirror and a place to work out. The mirror is vital. It functions as a critic, your personal instructor. If you're honest, the mirror will be too. It will point out every mistake - telegraphing, sloppy footwork, poor body mechanics, and even lack of physical conditioning.

Proper shadowboxing develops speed, power, balance, footwork, combination skills, sound form, and finesse. It even promotes a better understanding of the ranges of combat.

As you progress, you can incorporate light dumbbells into shadowboxing workouts to enhance power and speed. Start off with one to three pounds and gradually work your way up.

Once again, interval training with shadowboxing requires you to alternate drills after every round. For example, your first round would include heavy bag training, followed by a round of shadowboxing, then heavy bag training, and so on.

What follows are a few interval workout routines featuring heavy bag training and shadowboxing.

Heavy Bag Bible

Beginner Level
Interval Workout Routine (Shadowboxing)

Round	Activity	Duration of Each Round	Rest Period
1	Heavy Bag	1 minute	2 minutes
2	Shadowboxing	2 minutes	1 minute
3	Heavy Bag	2 minutes	2 minutes
4	Shadowboxing	1 minute	1 minute
5	Heavy Bag	2 minutes	2 minutes
6	Shadowboxing	2 minutes	1 minute
7	Heavy Bag	1 minute	2 minutes
8	Shadowboxing	1 minute	1 minute

Book Three: Heavy Bag Workout

Intermediate Level
Interval Workout Routine (Shadowboxing)

Round	Activity	Duration of Each Round	Rest Period
1	Heavy Bag	2 minutes	2 minutes
2	Shadowboxing	2 minutes	1 minute
3	Heavy Bag	2 minutes	2 minutes
4	Shadowboxing	2 minutes	1 minute
5	Heavy Bag	2 minutes	2 minutes
6	Shadowboxing	2 minutes	1 minute
7	Heavy Bag	2 minutes	2 minutes
8	Shadowboxing	2 minutes	1 minute
9	Heavy Bag	2 minutes	2 minutes
10	Shadowboxing	2 minutes	2 minutes

Heavy Bag Bible

Advanced Level
Interval Workout Routine (Shadowboxing)

Round	Activity	Duration of Each Round	Rest Period
1	Heavy Bag	2 minutes	2 minutes
2	Shadowboxing	2 minutes	1 minute
3	Heavy Bag	3 minutes	2 minutes
4	Shadowboxing	3 minutes	1 minute
5	Heavy Bag	3 minutes	2 minutes
6	Shadowboxing	3 minutes	1 minute
7	Heavy Bag	3 minutes	2 minutes
8	Shadowboxing	3 minutes	1 minute
9	Heavy Bag	3 minutes	2 minutes
10	Shadowboxing	3 minutes	2 minutes
11	Heavy Bag	3 minutes	2 minutes
12	Shadowboxing	3 minutes	2 minutes

If you really want to challenge yourself, consider shadowboxing with a weight vest. This will strengthen your entire body, including your cardiovascular system.

Double-End Bag Integration

The double-end bag is a small, inflatable lightweight bag constructed of vinyl or leather. It is suspended in the air using a durable elastic bungee cord that anchors it to the ceiling and the floor.

This unique piece of equipment allows you to develop both offensive and defensive fighting skills. What follows is a brief list a fighting attributes that can be developed:

- Improves punching accuracy.
- Improves offensive timing.
- Improves punching speed.
- Improves eye-hand coordination.
- Develops counterpunching skills.
- Develops defensive techniques such as slipping skills.
- Improves reflexes.
- Develops cardiovascular endurance
- Develops punching endurance.
- Develops punching combination skills.

The double-end bag also comes in three different sizes including large, medium and small. The smaller the bag, the more challenging it is to hit. As a rule of thumb, beginners should always start off with a large size bag.

Heavy Bag Bible

Here are a few interval workout routines featuring both the heavy bag and double-end bag.

Beginner Level
Interval Workout Routine (Double-end bag)

Round	Activity	Duration of Each Round	Rest Period
1	Heavy Bag	1 minute	2 minutes
2	Double-end bag	2 minutes	1 minute
3	Heavy Bag	2 minutes	2 minutes
4	Double-end bag	1 minute	1 minute
5	Heavy Bag	2 minutes	2 minutes
6	Double-end bag	2 minutes	1 minute
7	Heavy Bag	1 minute	2 minutes
8	Double-end bag	1 minute	1 minute

Intermediate Level
Interval Workout Routine (Double-end bag)

Round	Activity	Duration of Each Round	Rest Period
1	Heavy Bag	2 minutes	2 minutes
2	Double-end bag	2 minutes	1 minute
3	Heavy Bag	2 minutes	2 minutes
4	Double-end bag	2 minutes	1 minute
5	Heavy Bag	2 minutes	2 minutes
6	Double-end bag	2 minutes	1 minute
7	Heavy Bag	2 minutes	2 minutes
8	Double-end bag	2 minutes	1 minute
9	Heavy Bag	2 minutes	2 minutes
10	Double-end bag	2 minutes	2 minutes

The double-end bag requires considerable practice and a lot of patience. In fact, it is probably one of the most difficult pieces of training equipment to master.

Advanced Level
Interval Workout Routine (Double-end-bag)

Round	Activity	Duration of Each Round	Rest Period
1	Heavy Bag	2 minutes	2 minutes
2	Double-end bag	2 minutes	1 minute
3	Heavy Bag	3 minutes	2 minutes
4	Double-end bag	3 minutes	1 minute
5	Heavy Bag	3 minutes	2 minutes
6	Double-end bag	3 minutes	1 minute
7	Heavy Bag	3 minutes	2 minutes
8	Double-end bag	3 minutes	1 minute
9	Heavy Bag	3 minutes	2 minutes
10	Double-end bag	3 minutes	2 minutes
11	Heavy Bag	3 minutes	2 minutes
12	Double-end bag	3 minutes	2 minutes

To properly control the movement of the double-end bag, you must always hit it directly in the center. If you don't it will bounce uncontrollably to the right and left.

Focus Mitt Integration

The focus mitt (or punching mitt) is an exceptional piece of equipment that can be used by just about anyone. It develops punching speed, rhythm, endurance, accuracy, timing, reflexes, footwork, punching combinations, and counterpunching techniques.

By placing the mitts at various angles and levels, you can perform every conceivable kick, punch, or strike know to man. Properly utilized, focus mitts will refine your defensive reaction time and condition your entire body.

Focus mitts are constructed of durable leather designed to withstand tremendous punishment. Compared to other pieces of training equipment, the focus mitt is relatively inexpensive. However, an effective workout requires two mitts (one for each hand). You will also need a training partner (called the feeder) to hold the mitts. Your partner plays a vital role during your workouts by determining which combinations you will throw and their speed of delivery. In fact, the intensity of your workouts will depend largely upon his or her ability to manipulate the mitts and push you to your limit.

Heavy Bag Bible

To benefit from any focus-mitt workout, you must learn to concentrate intensely throughout the entire session. Block out all distractions. Try to visualize the mitt as a living, breathing opponent, not an inanimate target. This type of visualization will make all the difference in your training.

Here are few sample interval routines integrating the heavy bag with the focus mitts.

Beginner Level
Interval Workout Routine (Focus Mitts)

Round	Activity	Duration of Each Round	Rest Period
1	Heavy Bag	1 minute	2 minutes
2	Focus Mitts	2 minutes	1 minute
3	Heavy Bag	2 minutes	2 minutes
4	Focus Mitts	1 minute	1 minute
5	Heavy Bag	2 minutes	2 minutes
6	Focus Mitts	2 minutes	1 minute
7	Heavy Bag	1 minute	2 minutes
8	Focus Mitts	1 minute	1 minute

Book Three: Heavy Bag Workout

Intermediate Level
Interval Workout Routine (Focus Mitts)

Round	Activity	Duration of Each Round	Rest Period
1	Heavy Bag	2 minutes	2 minutes
2	Focus Mitts	2 minutes	1 minute
3	Heavy Bag	2 minutes	2 minutes
4	Focus Mitts	2 minutes	1 minute
5	Heavy Bag	2 minutes	2 minutes
6	Focus Mitts	2 minutes	1 minute
7	Heavy Bag	2 minutes	2 minutes
8	Focus Mitts	2 minutes	1 minute
9	Heavy Bag	2 minutes	2 minutes
10	Focus Mitts	2 minutes	2 minutes

I often tell my students that a good focus mitt feeder is one step ahead of his training partner, whereas a great focus mitt feeder is two steps ahead of his partner.

Advanced Level
Interval Workout Routine (Focus Mitts)

Round	Activity	Duration of Each Round	Rest Period
1	Heavy Bag	2 minutes	2 minutes
2	Focus Mitts	2 minutes	1 minute
3	Heavy Bag	3 minutes	2 minutes
4	Focus Mitts	3 minutes	1 minute
5	Heavy Bag	3 minutes	2 minutes
6	Focus Mitts	3 minutes	1 minute
7	Heavy Bag	3 minutes	2 minutes
8	Focus Mitts	3 minutes	1 minute
9	Heavy Bag	3 minutes	2 minutes
10	Focus Mitts	3 minutes	2 minutes
11	Heavy Bag	3 minutes	2 minutes
12	Focus Mitts	3 minutes	2 minutes

Unlike the heavy bag, the focus mitts are more forgiving on your wrists and hands and will allow you to progressively build up your power as your punching form improves.

Book Three: Heavy Bag Workout

Speed Bag Integration

The speed is used by boxers to develop coordination, endurance, timing, and rhythm. However, let me go on the record and state that I'm not a big fan of the speed bag. In fact, I believe it's an antiquated training tool that develops bad habits. Some include the following:

1. **Centerline exposure** - in order to strike the speed bag effectively, you must stand squarely in front of the bag. This means you must sacrifice your fighting stance and completely expose your centerline.

2. **Unrealistic attack rhythm** - the impact rhythm generated on a speed bag isn't remotely close to the attack rhythms used in real fighting.

3. **Improper fist positioning** - the speed bag requires you to *roll* your fists and strike it with the edge of your hands. If you would never punch this way in a real fight, then why on earth would you train this way?

4. **Poor body mechanics** - to maintain a fast striking rhythm on the bag, you must abandon proper punching mechanics.

5. **Mobility limitation** - since the speed bag is attached to a platform, your movement is significantly restricted. In fact, you must stay in close contact with the bag at all times.

6. **Lack of power** - to maintain the proper striking rhythm on the bag, you must only hit it with a slight amount of force. This style of punching is impractical for both the boxing ring and the street.

Nevertheless, I'm including the speed bag in this section out of respect for the boxing purist who insists on adding it to their training.

Heavy Bag Bible

Beginner Level
Interval Workout Routine (Speed Bag)

Round	Activity	Duration of Each Round	Rest Period
1	Heavy Bag	1 minute	2 minutes
2	Speed Bag	2 minutes	1 minute
3	Heavy Bag	2 minutes	2 minutes
4	Speed Bag	1 minute	1 minute
5	Heavy Bag	2 minutes	2 minutes
6	Speed Bag	2 minutes	1 minute
7	Heavy Bag	1 minute	2 minutes
8	Speed Bag	1 minute	1 minute

When it comes to preparing for the ring or the street, remember to train the way you want to fight and fight the way you train!

Book Three: Heavy Bag Workout

Intermediate Level
Interval Workout Routine (Speed Bag)

Round	Activity	Duration of Each Round	Rest Period
1	Heavy Bag	2 minutes	2 minutes
2	Speed Bag	2 minutes	1 minute
3	Heavy Bag	2 minutes	2 minutes
4	Speed Bag	2 minutes	1 minute
5	Heavy Bag	2 minutes	2 minutes
6	Speed Bag	2 minutes	1 minute
7	Heavy Bag	2 minutes	2 minutes
8	Speed Bag	2 minutes	1 minute
9	Heavy Bag	2 minutes	2 minutes
10	Speed Bag	2 minutes	2 minutes

Remember to tighten your fists upon impact with bag. This action will allow your punches to travel with optimum speed and efficiency, and it will also augment the impact power of your strike.

Advanced Level
Interval Workout Routine (Speed Bag)

Round	Activity	Duration of Each Round	Rest Period
1	Heavy Bag	2 minutes	2 minutes
2	Speed Bag	2 minutes	1 minute
3	Heavy Bag	3 minutes	2 minutes
4	Speed Bag	3 minutes	1 minute
5	Heavy Bag	3 minutes	2 minutes
6	Speed Bag	3 minutes	1 minute
7	Heavy Bag	3 minutes	2 minutes
8	Speed Bag	3 minutes	1 minute
9	Heavy Bag	3 minutes	2 minutes
10	Speed Bag	3 minutes	2 minutes
11	Heavy Bag	3 minutes	2 minutes
12	Speed Bag	3 minutes	2 minutes

Book Three: Heavy Bag Workout

Workout Routine #12
Bare-Knuckle Training

While bag gloves are essential for protecting your hands when training, every once in a while you should workout without them. In fact, this type of bare-knuckle training is critical to anyone interested in reality-based self-defense training.

As I have stated in many of my other books, in the streets you don't have the luxury of rules, regulations or protective equipment. You have to make due with what you have at the moment of a high-risk self-defense encounter. Bare-knuckle training will help prepare you for the real thing. In fact, striking the heavy bag without hand protection is essential because it conditions your hands, knuckles, tendons, and joints for the rigors of street fighting.

However, bare-knuckle bag training is very hard on your wrists, hands, and knuckles. Transitioning from hand protected training

453

Heavy Bag Bible

to bare-knuckles is not easy. Initially, punching bare-fisted will feel awkward to even the most experienced fighter. Therefore, it's imperative to start out with approximately 25% of you punching power and increase it over a period of time.

Bare-knuckle training should only be performed on vinyl or soft leather bags. Do not use canvas heavy bags, they are made or coarse material that will lacerate your fingers and knuckles and permanently stain your heavy bag with blood.

One of the best ways to condition your hands and wrists for bare-knuckle fighting is to practice my *glove on/glove off* program. Essentially, you are going to alternate between bare handed and gloved punching. After several months, you can progress to exclusively bare-knuckle training.

What follows are several *glove on/glove off* workout routines.

Bare-knuckle fighting is a skill set that's much different from boxing and other combat sports. In fact, I know of several stories where professional boxers have broken their hands during a bare handed fist fight. This is because most professional fighters don't condition their hands for this type of fighting.

Book Three: Heavy Bag Workout

Beginner Level
Bare-Knuckle Training (Glove On/Glove Off)

Round	Activity	Duration of Each Round	Rest Period
1	Glove on	1 minute	2 minutes
2	Glove off	30 seconds	1 minute
3	Glove on	2 minutes	2 minutes
4	Glove off	45 seconds	1 minute
5	Glove on	2 minutes	2 minutes
6	Glove off	1 minute	1 minute
7	Glove on	2 minutes	2 minutes
8	Glove off	90 seconds	1 minute

If bare-knuckle bag training is too hard on your hands, consider hitting the focus mitts instead. Unlike the heavy bag, the punching mitts are more forgiving on your knuckles.

Intermediate Level
Bare-Knuckle Training (Glove On/Glove Off)

Round	Activity	Duration of Each Round	Rest Period
1	Glove on	2 minutes	2 minutes
2	Glove off	1 minute	1 minute
3	Glove on	2 minutes	2 minutes
4	Glove off	90 seconds	1 minute
5	Glove on	2 minutes	2 minutes
6	Glove off	90 seconds	1 minute
7	Glove on	2 minutes	2 minutes
8	Glove off	2 minutes	1 minute
9	Glove on	2 minutes	2 minutes
10	Glove off	2 minutes	2 minutes

To avoid potential hand problems, don't perform bare-knuckle training more than three times per month.

Book Three: Heavy Bag Workout

Advanced Level
Bare-Knuckle Training (Glove On/Glove Off)

Round	Activity	Duration of Each Round	Rest Period
1	Glove on	2 minutes	2 minutes
2	Glove off	2 minutes	1 minute
3	Glove on	3 minutes	2 minutes
4	Glove off	2 minutes	1 minute
5	Glove on	3 minutes	2 minutes
6	Glove off	2 1/2 minutes	1 minute
7	Glove on	3 minutes	2 minutes
8	Glove off	2 1/2 minutes	1 minute
9	Glove on	3 minutes	2 minutes
10	Glove off	3 minutes	2 minutes
11	Glove on	3 minutes	2 minutes
12	Glove off	3 minutes	2 minutes

Proper breathing is one of the most important and often neglected aspects of bag work. Proper breathing promotes muscular relaxation and increases the speed and efficiency of your combinations. The rate at which you breathe will also determine how quickly your cardiorespiratory system can recover from a round.

Heavy Bag Bible

Workout Routine #13
Pummel Training

Pummel training is designed for both mixed martial arts and street self-defense training. It requires you to attack the heavy bag from the top mounted position for specified period of time.

There are two punches that can be delivered from the mount position. They are:

- **Linear blast**
- **Short Arc Hammer Fist**

When performing both punches, remember to keep everything tight and aim for the center of the bag. Your objective is to punch through your target. When pummeling the heavy bag, you can vary the cadence of your punches from moderate to full speed.

Warning! Pummeling is a devastating self-defense technique that

Book Three: Heavy Bag Workout

can severely injure your adversary and should only be used in life and death situations. Remember to always be certain that your actions are legally and morally justified in the eyes of the law.

To execute the pummel drill, apply the following steps:

1. Place a heavy bag on the floor.

2. Have your training partner tie a rope (approximately five feet long) to the top of the bag.

3. Mount the heavy bag (the same way you would mount an assailant in a ground fight).

4. Employ full-speed, full-force strikes on the upper portion of the heavy bag. Be vicious and attack the bag with all of the aggression you can muster.

5. Have your training partner pull vigorously (side to side, and up and down) on the rope while you deliver the blows. Strive to maintain a good base and avoid losing your balance when your partner tugs the bag.

6. Perform this drill for a minimum of five rounds.

The pummeling drill is conducted for a prolonged amount of time. This is done strictly for body mechanic mastery and muscular endurance. Never apply pummeling on a human being for a prolonged amount of time. Doing so can cause brain damage or death.

Pummeling Demonstration

Step 1: The practitioner begins by throwing a left punch from the top mounted position.

Step 2: He immediately follows with a right punch.

Book Three: Heavy Bag Workout

Step 3: He throws another left punch.

Step 4: Then another right.

Heavy Bag Bible

Step 5: Followed by a left.

Step 6: He continues punching for a total of two minutes.

Beginner Level Pummel Drill

Round	Duration of Each Round	Rest Period
1	30 seconds	2 minutes
2	45 seconds	2 minutes
3	45 seconds	2 minutes
4	1 minute	2 minutes
5	1 minute	2 minutes
6	1 minute	2 minutes
7	1 minute	2 minutes
8	1 minute	2 minutes

Heavy Bag Bible

Intermediate Level Pummel Drill

Round	Duration of Each Round	Rest Period
1	1 minute	2 minutes
2	90 seconds	1 minute
3	2 minutes	2 minutes
4	2 minutes	1 minute
5	90 seconds	2 minutes
6	2 1/2 minutes	1 minute
7	2 minutes	2 minutes
8	1 minute	1 minute
9	3 minutes	2 minutes
10	3 minutes	2 minutes

Advanced Level Pummel Drill

Round	Duration of Each Round	Rest Period
1	2 minutes	2 minutes
2	2 minutes	1 minute
3	3 minutes	2 minutes
4	2 minutes	1 minute
5	3 minutes	2 minutes
6	2 1/2 minutes	1 minute
7	3 minutes	2 minutes
8	2 1/2 minutes	1 minute
9	3 minutes	2 minutes
10	3 minutes	2 minutes
11	4 minutes	2 minutes
12	4 minutes	2 minutes

Workout Routine #14
Impairment Training

Impairment training teaches you how to fight when temporarily injured or impaired. There are several different types of impairment training routines you can perform on the heavy bag. Let's take a look at one of them.

Disorientation Drill

The Disorientation drill replicates the lightheaded sensation you will feel when you get hit by the opponent. This exercise is particularly useful because it teaches you to continue fighting when you are dizzy and lose your balance during a fight. To perform the exercise, employ the following steps:

1. Start with both your hands at your sides and your head looking down at the floor.

Book Three: Heavy Bag Workout

2. Next, close your eyes and begin spinning your body in a clockwise direction.
3. Continue spinning for approximately 10 seconds.
4. After 10 seconds, your training partner calls out "fight!"
5. Immediately stop spinning, open your eyes and attack the heavy bag with a barrage of punching combinations. Remember, you're going to be very dizzy, so do your best to maintain proper punching form.
6. Continue punching the heavy bag for approximately 20 seconds.
7. Rest for a minimum of 5 minutes before going again.

Disorientation Drill Demonstration

Step 1: The practitioner begins with his head down, eyes closed, and his arms at his sides.

Heavy Bag Bible

Step 2: The time keeper instructs him to begin spinning.

Step 3: The man starts to spin his body in a clockwise direction.

Book Three: Heavy Bag Workout

Step 4: He continues to spin with his eyes closed for approximately 10 seconds.

Step 5: At the end of 10 seconds, the time keeper yells, "fight!"

Heavy Bag Bible

Step 6: The practitioner immediately opens his eyes and tries to balance himself.

Step 7: He moves toward the bag.

Book Three: Heavy Bag Workout

Step 8: Despite his dizziness, he begins punching the heavy bag.

Step 9: After his second punch, the drill takes effect.

Heavy Bag Bible

Step 10: The practitioner loses his balance.

Step 11: And falls to side.

Book Three: Heavy Bag Workout

Step 12: He crashes into the wall.

Step 13: He quickly regains his balance and goes after the bag once more.

Heavy Bag Bible

Step 14: He resumes punching the heavy bag.

Step 15: He continues hitting the bag for approximately 20 seconds.

Book Three: Heavy Bag Workout

Step 16: The practitioner is clearly disoriented at the completion of the drill.

Be very careful when practicing the disorientation drill. Make certain your training area is away from windows, glass doors objects, children, and pets.

Heavy Bag Bible

Disorientation Drill Workout Routines

Skill Level	Duration of Spin	Duration of Punching Round	Rest Period Between Rounds	Total Number of rounds
Beginner	5 seconds	10 seconds	10 minutes	2
Beginner	5 seconds	12 seconds	10 minutes	2
Beginner	8 seconds	14 seconds	10 minutes	2
Beginner	8 seconds	15 seconds	10 minutes	2
Intermediate	10 seconds	15 seconds	5 minutes	3
Intermediate	10 seconds	20 seconds	5 minutes	3
Intermediate	10 seconds	20 seconds	5 minutes	3
Intermediate	10 seconds	25 seconds	5 minutes	3
Advanced	10 seconds	25 seconds	5 minutes	4
Advanced	10 seconds	30 seconds	5 minutes	4
Advanced	10 seconds	45 seconds	5 minutes	4
Advanced	10 seconds	45 seconds	5 minutes	4

Other Impairment Drills

There are many other impairment drills that you can perform. Here are a few suggestions that will get you started.

1. Workout on the heavy bag with one arm in a sling.
2. Wear an eye patch and see how it affects your punching skills.
3. Train when you are suffering from a hangover.
4. Wear a weight vest when training.
5. Wear an elevation training mask when working out on the heavy bag.
6. Want to experience some real physical discomfort, try working out on the bag with a marble in your shoe.
7. To replicate unstable terrain, workout with sand, gravel or sawdust on the floor (be careful).
8. Practice hitting the bag with a light source beaming into your face.
9. Workout under poor lighting conditions.
10. Be creative, you are only limited by your imagination.

Heavy Bag Bible

Heavy Bag Resources

Heavy Bag Videos

If you wish to explore additional information about heavy bag training, I encourage you to check out the following video and book resources. Instructional videos include the following:

- *Heavy Bag Training*
- *Punching Bag Combinations*

Heavy Bag Training DVD

Punching Bag Combinations DVD

Heavy Bag Books

The entire heavy bag training book series is also available in both paperback and kindle editions.

Heavy Bag Training
Book #1

Heavy Bag Combinations
Book #2

Heavy Bag Workout
Book #3

Appendix

Heavy Bag Bible

Foundational Heavy Bag Skills

In this section, I am going to teach you the foundational fighting techniques required to perform all of the heavy bag workout routines featured in this book. These basic skills include the fighting stance, footwork, jab, rear cross, hooks and uppercuts. Let's begin with the fighting stance..

The Fighting Stance

The fighting stance defines your ability to execute both offensive and defensive techniques, and it will play a material role in the outcome of a fight. It stresses strategic soundness and simplicity over complexity and style. The fighting stance also facilitates optimum execution of your body weapons while simultaneously protecting your vital targets against quick counter strikes.

The fighting stance is designed around the centerline. The centerline is an imaginary vertical line running through the center of the body, from the top of your head to the bottom of the groin. Most of your vital targets are situated along this line, including the head, throat, solar plexus, and groin. Obviously, you want to avoid directly exposing your centerline to the assailant. To achieve this, position your feet and body at a 45-degree angle

Pictured here, a left lead fighting stance.

from the opponent. This moves your body targets back and away from direct strikes but leaves you strategically positioned to attack.

When assuming a fighting stance, place your strongest and most coordinated side forward. For example, a right-handed person stands with his or her right side toward the assailant. Keeping your strongest side forward enhances the speed, power, and accuracy of your strike. This doesn't mean that you should never practice fighting from your other side. You must be capable of fighting from both sides, and you should spend equal practice time on the left and right stances.

Many people make the costly mistake of stepping forward to assume a fighting stance. Do not do this! This action only moves you closer to your assailant before your protective structure is soundly established. Moving closer to your assailant also dramatically reduces your defensive reaction time. So get into the habit of stepping backward to assume your stance. Practice this daily until it becomes a natural and economical movement.

How to Assume a Fighting Stance

When assuming your fighting stance, place your feet about shoulder width apart. Keep your knees bent and flexible. Think of your legs as power springs to launch you through the ranges of unarmed combat (kicking, punching, and grappling range).

Mobility is also important, as we'll discuss later. All footwork and strategic movement should be performed on the balls of your feet. Your weight distribution is also an important factor. Since combat is dynamic, your weight distribution will frequently change. However, when stationary, keep 50 percent of your body weight on each leg and always be in control of it.

The hands are aligned one behind the other along your centerline. The lead arm is held high and bent at approximately 90 degrees. The rear arm is kept back by the chin. Arranged this way, the hands not

Heavy Bag Bible

only protect the upper centerline but also allow quick deployment of your body weapons. When holding your guard, do not tighten your shoulder or arm muscles prior to striking. Stay relaxed and loose. Finally, keep your chin slightly angled down. This diminishes target size and reduces the likelihood of a paralyzing blow to your chin or a lethal strike to your throat.

The best method for practicing your fighting stance is in front of a full-length mirror. Place the mirror in an area that allows sufficient room for movement; a garage or basement is perfect. Stand in front of the mirror, far enough away to see your entire body. Stand naturally with your arms relaxed at your sides. Now close your eyes and quickly assume your fighting stance. Open your eyes and check for flaws. Look for low hand guards, improper foot positioning or body angle, rigid shoulders and knees, etc. Drill this way repeatedly, working from both the right and left side. Practice this until your fighting stance becomes second nature.

Footwork & Mobility

Next are footwork and mobility. I define mobility as the ability to move your body quickly and freely, which is accomplished through basic footwork. The safest footwork involves quick, economical steps performed on the balls of your feet, while you remain relaxed and balanced. Keep in mind that balance is your most important consideration.

Basic footwork can be used for both offensive and defensive purposes, and it is structured around four general directions: forward, backward, right, and left. However, always remember this footwork rule of thumb: Always move the foot closest to the direction you want to go first, and let the other foot follow an equal distance. This prevents cross-stepping, which can cost you your life in a high-risk combat situation.

Appendix

Basic Footwork Movements

1. Moving forward (advance)- from your fighting stance, first move your front foot forward (approximately 12 inches) and then move your rear foot an equal distance.

2. Moving backward (retreat) - from your fighting stance, first move your rear foot backward (approximately 12 inches) and then move your front foot an equal distance.

3. Moving right (sidestep right) - from your fighting stance, first move your right foot to the right (approximately 12 inches) and then move your left foot an equal distance.

4. Moving left (sidestep left) - from your fighting stance, first move your left foot to the left (approximately 12 inches) and then move your right foot an equal distance.

Practice these four movements for 10 to 15 minutes a day in front of a full-length mirror. In a couple weeks, your footwork should be quick, balanced, and natural.

Circling Right and Left

Strategic circling is an advanced form of footwork where you will use your front leg as a pivot point. This type of movement can also be used defensively to evade an overwhelming assault or to strike the opponent from various strategic angles. Strategic circling can be performed from either a left or right stance.

Circling left (from a left stance) - this means you'll be moving your body around the opponent in a clockwise direction. From a left stance, step 8 to 12 inches to the left with your left foot, then use your left leg as a pivot point and wheel your entire rear leg to the left until the correct stance and positioning is acquired.

Circling right (from a right stance) - from a right stance, step 8 to 12 inches to the right with your right foot, then use your right leg

Heavy Bag Bible

as a pivot point and wheel your entire rear leg to the right until the correct stance and positioning is acquired.

Punching Techniques

In this section, I'm going to teach you four different punching skills that you will be using during you heavy bag workouts. They are:

- **Jab**
- **Rear cross (aka Straight Right)**
- **Hook punch**
- **Uppercut punch**

The Jab

The jab is a linear punch thrown from your lead arm, and contact is made with the center knuckle. To execute the technique, perform the following steps.

1. Start off in a fighting stance with both of your hands held up in the guard position. Your fists should be lightly clenched with both of your elbows pointing to the ground.
2. Simultaneously step toward the opponent and twist your front waist and shoulder forward as you snap your front arm into the target.
3. When delivering the punch, remember not to lock out your arm as this will have a "pushing effect" on the target.
4. Quickly retract your arm back to the starting position.
5. One common mistake when throwing the punch is to let it deflect off to the side of the target. Also, keep in mind that jabs can be delivered to the opponent's head or body. Targets for the punch include the opponent's nose, chin, and solar plexus.

Appendix

Pictured here, the jab.

Rear Cross or Straight Right

The rear cross is considered the heavy artillery of punches and it's thrown from your rear arm. To execute the punch, perform the following steps:

1. Start off in a fighting stance with both of your hands held up in the guard position. Your fists should be lightly clenched with both of your elbows pointing to the ground.

2. Next, quickly twist your rear hips and shoulders forward as you snap your rear arm into the target. Proper waist twisting and weight transfer is of paramount importance to the rear cross. You must shift your weight from your rear foot to your lead leg as you throw the punch.

3. To maximize the impact of the punch, make certain that your fist is positioned horizontally. Avoid overextending the blow or exposing your chin during its execution.

Heavy Bag Bible

4. Once again, do not lock out your arm when throwing the punch. Let the power of the blow sink into the target before you retract it back to the starting position.

The rear cross.

Hook Punch

The hook is another devastating punch in your arsenal, yet it's also one of the most difficult to master. This punch can be performed from either your front or rear hand, and it can be delivered to both high or low targets.

1. Start in a fighting stance with your hand guard held up. Both of your elbows should be pointing to the ground, and your fists clenched loosely.

2. Next, quickly and smoothly, raise your elbow up so that your arm is parallel to the ground while simultaneously torquing your shoulder, hip, and foot into the direction of the blow.

3. When delivering the strike, be certain your arm is bent at least ninety degrees and that your wrist and forearm are kept

Appendix

straight throughout the movement.

4. As you throw the punch, your fist is positioned vertically. The elbow should be locked when contact is made with the target. Remember to simultaneously tighten your fists when impact is made with the target. This action will allow your punch to travel with optimum speed and efficiency, and it will also augment the impact power of your strike.

5. Return to the starting position.

The lead hook punch.

Uppercut Punch

The uppercut is a another powerful punch that can be delivered from both the lead and rear arm. To execute the blow, perform the following steps.

1. Start off in a fighting stance with both of your hands held up in the guard position. Your fists should be lightly clenched

Heavy Bag Bible

with both of your elbows pointing to the ground.
2. Next, drop your shoulder and bend your knees.
3. Quickly, stand up and drive your fist upward and into the target. Your palm should be facing you when contact is made with the target. To avoid any possible injury, always keep your wrists straight.
4. Make certain your punch has a tight arc. Avoid "winding up" the blow. A properly executed uppercut punch should be a tight explosive jolt.
5. Return to the fighting stance.

The rear uppercut.

Appendix

The lead uppercut punch.

Heavy Bag Bible

Glossary of Terms

The following terms are defined in the context of Contemporary Fighting Arts and its related concepts. In many instances, the definitions bear little resemblance to those found in a standard dictionary.

A

accuracy—The precise or exact projection of force. Accuracy is also defined as the ability to execute a combative movement with precision and exactness.

adaptability—The ability to physically and psychologically adjust to new or different conditions or circumstances of combat.

advanced first-strike tools—Offensive techniques that are specifically used when confronted with multiple opponents.

aerobic exercise—Literally, "with air." Exercise that elevates the heart rate to a training level for a prolonged period of time, usually 30 minutes.

affective preparedness – One of the three components of preparedness. Affective preparedness means being emotionally, philosophically, and spiritually prepared for the strains of combat. See cognitive preparedness and psychomotor preparedness.

aggression—Hostile and injurious behavior directed toward a person.

aggressive response—One of the three possible counters when assaulted by a grab, choke, or hold from a standing position. Aggressive response requires you to counter the enemy with destructive blows and strikes. See moderate response and passive response.

aggressive hand positioning—Placement of hands so as to imply aggressive or hostile intentions.

agility—An attribute of combat. One's ability to move his or her body quickly and gracefully.

amalgamation—A scientific process of uniting or merging.

ambidextrous—The ability to perform with equal facility on both the right and left sides of the body.

anabolic steroids – synthetic chemical compounds that resemble the male sex hormone testosterone. This performance-enhancing drug is known to increase lean muscle mass, strength, and endurance.

analysis and integration—One of the five elements of CFA's mental component. This is the painstaking process of breaking down various elements, concepts, sciences, and disciplines into their atomic parts, and then methodically and strategically analyzing, experimenting, and drastically modifying the information so that it fulfills three combative requirements: efficiency, effectiveness, and safety. Only then is it finally integrated into the CFA system.

anatomical striking targets—The various anatomical body targets that can be struck and which are especially vulnerable to potential harm. They include: the eyes, temple, nose, chin, back of neck, front of neck, solar plexus, ribs, groin, thighs, knees, shins, and instep.

anchoring – The strategic process of trapping the assailant's neck or limb in order to control the range of engagement during razing.

assailant—A person who threatens or attacks another person.

assault—The threat or willful attempt to inflict injury upon the person of another.

assault and battery—The unlawful touching of another person without justification.

assessment—The process of rapidly gathering, analyzing, and accurately evaluating information in terms of threat and danger. You

Glossary of Terms

can assess people, places, actions, and objects.

attack—Offensive action designed to physically control, injure, or kill another person.

attitude—One of the three factors that determine who wins a street fight. Attitude means being emotionally, philosophically, and spiritually liberated from societal and religious mores. See skills and knowledge.

attributes of combat—The physical, mental, and spiritual qualities that enhance combat skills and tactics.

awareness—Perception or knowledge of people, places, actions, and objects. (In CFA, there are three categories of tactical awareness: criminal awareness, situational awareness, and self-awareness.)

B

balance—One's ability to maintain equilibrium while stationary or moving.

blading the body—Strategically positioning your body at a 45-degree angle.

blitz and disengage—A style of sparring whereby a fighter moves into a range of combat, unleashes a strategic compound attack, and then quickly disengages to a safe distance. Of all sparring methodologies, the blitz and disengage most closely resembles a real street fight.

block—A defensive tool designed to intercept the assailant's attack by placing a non-vital target between the assailant's strike and your vital body target.

body composition—The ratio of fat to lean body tissue.

body language—Nonverbal communication through posture, gestures, and facial expressions.

The Heavy Bag Bible

body mechanics—Technically precise body movement during the execution of a body weapon, defensive technique, or other fighting maneuver.

body tackle – A tackle that occurs when your opponent haphazardly rushes forward and plows his body into yours.

body weapon—Also known as a tool, one of the various body parts that can be used to strike or otherwise injure or kill a criminal assailant.

burn out—A negative emotional state acquired by physically over- training. Some symptoms include: illness, boredom, anxiety, disinterest in training, and general sluggishness.

C

cadence—Coordinating tempo and rhythm to establish a timing pattern of movement.

cardiorespiratory conditioning—The component of physical fitness that deals with the heart, lungs, and circulatory system.

centerline—An imaginary vertical line that divides your body in half and which contains many of your vital anatomical targets.

choke holds—Holds that impair the flow of blood or oxygen to the brain.

circular movements—Movements that follow the direction of a curve.

close-quarter combat—One of the three ranges of knife and bludgeon combat. At this distance, you can strike, slash, or stab your assailant with a variety of close-quarter techniques.

cognitive development—One of the five elements of CFA's mental component. The process of developing and enhancing your fighting skills through specific mental exercises and techniques. See analysis

Glossary of Terms

and integration, killer instinct, philosophy, and strategic/tactical development.

cognitive exercises—Various mental exercises used to enhance fighting skills and tactics.

cognitive preparedness – One of the three components of preparedness. Cognitive preparedness means being equipped with the strategic concepts, principles, and general knowledge of combat. See affective preparedness and psychomotor preparedness.

combat-oriented training—Training that is specifically related to the harsh realities of both armed and unarmed combat. See ritual-oriented training and sport-oriented training.

combative arts—The various arts of war. See martial arts.

combative attributes—See attributes of combat.

combative fitness—A state characterized by cardiorespiratory and muscular/skeletal conditioning, as well as proper body composition.

combative mentality—Also known as the killer instinct, this is a combative state of mind necessary for fighting. See killer instinct.

combat ranges—The various ranges of unarmed combat.

combative utility—The quality of condition of being combatively useful.

combination(s)—See compound attack.

common peroneal nerve—A pressure point area located approximately four to six inches above the knee on the midline of the outside of the thigh.

composure—A combative attribute. Composure is a quiet and focused mind-set that enables you to acquire your combative agenda.

compound attack—One of the five conventional methods of attack. Two or more body weapons launched in strategic succession whereby the fighter overwhelms his assailant with a flurry of full speed, full-force blows.

conditioning training—A CFA training methodology requiring the practitioner to deliver a variety of offensive and defensive combinations for a 4-minute period. See proficiency training and street training.

contact evasion—Physically moving or manipulating your body to avoid being tackled by the adversary.

Contemporary Fighting Arts—A modern martial art and self-defense system made up of three parts: physical, mental, and spiritual.

conventional ground-fighting tools—Specific ground-fighting techniques designed to control, restrain, and temporarily incapacitate your adversary. Some conventional ground fighting tactics include: submission holds, locks, certain choking techniques, and specific striking techniques.

coordination—A physical attribute characterized by the ability to perform a technique or movement with efficiency, balance, and accuracy.

counterattack—Offensive action made to counter an assailant's initial attack.

courage—A combative attribute. The state of mind and spirit that enables a fighter to face danger and vicissitudes with confidence, resolution, and bravery.

creatine monohydrate—A tasteless and odorless white powder that mimics some of the effects of anabolic steroids. Creatine is a safe body-building product that can benefit anyone who wants to increase their strength, endurance, and lean muscle mass.

criminal awareness—One of the three categories of CFA awareness. It involves a general understanding and knowledge of the

Glossary of Terms

nature and dynamics of a criminal's motivations, mentalities, methods, and capabilities to perpetrate violent crime. See situational awareness and self-awareness.

criminal justice—The study of criminal law and the procedures associated with its enforcement.

criminology—The scientific study of crime and criminals.

cross-stepping—The process of crossing one foot in front of or behind the other when moving.

crushing tactics—Nuclear grappling-range techniques designed to crush the assailant's anatomical targets.

D

deadly force—Weapons or techniques that may result in unconsciousness, permanent disfigurement, or death.

deception—A combative attribute. A stratagem whereby you delude your assailant.

decisiveness—A combative attribute. The ability to follow a tactical course of action that is unwavering and focused.

defense—The ability to strategically thwart an assailant's attack (armed or unarmed).

defensive flow—A progression of continuous defensive responses.

defensive mentality—A defensive mind-set.

defensive reaction time—The elapsed time between an assailant's physical attack and your defensive response to that attack. See offensive reaction time.

demeanor—A person's outward behavior. One of the essential factors to consider when assessing a threatening individual.

diet—A lifestyle of healthy eating.

disingenuous vocalization—The strategic and deceptive utilization of words to successfully launch a preemptive strike at your adversary.

distancing—The ability to quickly understand spatial relationships and how they relate to combat.

distractionary tactics—Various verbal and physical tactics designed to distract your adversary.

double-end bag—A small leather ball hung from the ceiling and anchored to the floor with bungee cord. It helps develop striking accuracy, speed, timing, eye-hand coordination, footwork and overall defensive skills.

double-leg takedown—A takedown that occurs when your opponent shoots for both of your legs to force you to the ground.

E

ectomorph—One of the three somatotypes. A body type characterized by a high degree of slenderness, angularity, and fragility. See endomorph and mesomorph.

effectiveness—One of the three criteria for a CFA body weapon, technique, tactic, or maneuver. It means the ability to produce a desired effect. See efficiency and safety.

efficiency—One of the three criteria for a CFA body weapon, technique, tactic, or maneuver. It means the ability to reach an objective quickly and economically. See effectiveness and safety.

emotionless—A combative attribute. Being temporarily devoid of human feeling.

endomorph—One of the three somatotypes. A body type characterized by a high degree of roundness, softness, and body fat. See ectomorph and mesomorph.

evasion—A defensive maneuver that allows you to strategically

Glossary of Terms

maneuver your body away from the assailant's strike.

evasive sidestepping—Evasive footwork where the practitioner moves to either the right or left side.

evasiveness—A combative attribute. The ability to avoid threat or danger.

excessive force—An amount of force that exceeds the need for a particular event and is unjustified in the eyes of the law.

experimentation—The painstaking process of testing a combative hypothesis or theory.

explosiveness—A combative attribute that is characterized by a sudden outburst of violent energy.

F

fear—A strong and unpleasant emotion caused by the anticipation or awareness of threat or danger. There are three stages of fear in order of intensity: fright, panic, and terror. See fright, panic, and terror.

feeder—A skilled technician who manipulates the focus mitts.

femoral nerve—A pressure point area located approximately 6 inches above the knee on the inside of the thigh.

fighting stance—Any one of the stances used in CFA's system. A strategic posture you can assume when face-to-face with an unarmed assailant(s). The fighting stance is generally used after you have launched your first-strike tool.

fight-or-flight syndrome—A response of the sympathetic nervous system to a fearful and threatening situation, during which it prepares your body to either fight or flee from the perceived danger.

finesse—A combative attribute. The ability to skillfully execute a movement or a series of movements with grace and refinement.

first strike—Proactive force used to interrupt the initial stages of an assault before it becomes a self-defense situation.

first-strike principle—A CFA principle that states that when physical danger is imminent and you have no other tactical option but to fight back, you should strike first, strike fast, and strike with authority and keep the pressure on.

first-strike stance—One of the stances used in CFA's system. A strategic posture used prior to initiating a first strike.

first-strike tools—Specific offensive tools designed to initiate a preemptive strike against your adversary.

fisted blows – Hand blows delivered with a clenched fist.

five tactical options – The five strategic responses you can make in a self-defense situation, listed in order of increasing level of resistance: comply, escape, de-escalate, assert, and fight back.

flexibility—The muscles' ability to move through maximum natural ranges. See muscular/skeletal conditioning.

focus mitts—Durable leather hand mitts used to develop and sharpen offensive and defensive skills.

footwork—Quick, economical steps performed on the balls of the feet while you are relaxed, alert, and balanced. Footwork is structured around four general movements: forward, backward, right, and left.

fractal tool—Offensive or defensive tools that can be used in more than one combat range.

fright—The first stage of fear; quick and sudden fear. See panic and terror.

full Beat – One of the four beat classifications in the Widow Maker Program. The full beat strike has a complete initiation and retraction phase.

Glossary of Terms

G

going postal - a slang term referring to a person who suddenly and unexpectedly attacks you with an explosive and frenzied flurry of blows. Also known as postal attack.

grappling range—One of the three ranges of unarmed combat. Grappling range is the closest distance of unarmed combat from which you can employ a wide variety of close-quarter tools and techniques. The grappling range of unarmed combat is also divided into two planes: vertical (standing) and horizontal (ground fighting). See kicking range and punching range.

grappling-range tools—The various body tools and techniques that are employed in the grappling range of unarmed combat, including head butts; biting, tearing, clawing, crushing, and gouging tactics; foot stomps, horizontal, vertical, and diagonal elbow strikes, vertical and diagonal knee strikes, chokes, strangles, joint locks, and holds. See punching range tools and kicking range tools.

ground fighting—Also known as the horizontal grappling plane, this is fighting that takes place on the ground.

guard—Also known as the hand guard, this refers to a fighter's hand positioning.

guard position—Also known as leg guard or scissors hold, this is a ground-fighting position in which a fighter is on his back holding his opponent between his legs.

H

half beat - One of the four beat classifications in the Widow Maker Program. The half beat strike is delivered through the retraction phase of the proceeding strike.

hand positioning—See guard.

hand wraps—Long strips of cotton that are wrapped around the hands and wrists for greater protection.

haymaker—A wild and telegraphed swing of the arms executed by an unskilled fighter.

head-hunter—A fighter who primarily attacks the head.

heavy bag—A large cylindrical bag used to develop kicking, punching, or striking power.

high-line kick—One of the two different classifications of a kick. A kick that is directed to targets above an assailant's waist level. See low-line kick.

hip fusing—A full-contact drill that teaches a fighter to "stand his ground" and overcome the fear of exchanging blows with a stronger opponent. This exercise is performed by connecting two fighters with a 3-foot chain, forcing them to fight in the punching range of unarmed combat.

histrionics—The field of theatrics or acting.

hook kick—A circular kick that can be delivered in both kicking and punching ranges.

hook punch—A circular punch that can be delivered in both the punching and grappling ranges.

I

impact power—Destructive force generated by mass and velocity.

impact training—A training exercise that develops pain tolerance.

incapacitate—To disable an assailant by rendering him unconscious or damaging his bones, joints, or organs.

initiative—Making the first offensive move in combat.

inside position—The area between the opponent's arms, where he

Glossary of Terms

has the greatest amount of control.

intent—One of the essential factors to consider when assessing a threatening individual. The assailant's purpose or motive. See demeanor, positioning, range, and weapon capability.

intuition—The innate ability to know or sense something without the use of rational thought.

J

jersey Pull – Strategically pulling the assailant's shirt or jacket over his head as he disengages from the clinch position.

joint lock—A grappling-range technique that immobilizes the assailant's joint.

K

kick—A sudden, forceful strike with the foot.

kicking range—One of the three ranges of unarmed combat. Kicking range is the furthest distance of unarmed combat wherein you use your legs to strike an assailant. See grappling range and punching range.

kicking-range tools—The various body weapons employed in the kicking range of unarmed combat, including side kicks, push kicks, hook kicks, and vertical kicks.

killer instinct—A cold, primal mentality that surges to your consciousness and turns you into a vicious fighter.

kinesics—The study of nonlinguistic body movement communications. (For example, eye movement, shrugs, or facial gestures.)

kinesiology—The study of principles and mechanics of human movement.

kinesthetic perception—The ability to accurately feel your body during the execution of a particular movement.

knowledge—One of the three factors that determine who will win a street fight. Knowledge means knowing and understanding how to fight. See skills and attitude.

L

lead side -The side of the body that faces an assailant.

leg guard—See guard position.

linear movement—Movements that follow the path of a straight line.

low-maintenance tool—Offensive and defensive tools that require the least amount of training and practice to maintain proficiency. Low maintenance tools generally do not require preliminary stretching.

low-line kick—One of the two different classifications of a kick. A kick that is directed to targets below the assailant's waist level. (See high-line kick.)

lock—See joint lock.

M

maneuver—To manipulate into a strategically desired position.

MAP—An acronym that stands for moderate, aggressive, passive. MAP provides the practitioner with three possible responses to various grabs, chokes, and holds that occur from a standing position. See aggressive response, moderate response, and passive response.

martial arts—The "arts of war."

masking—The process of concealing your true feelings from your opponent by manipulating and managing your body language.

mechanics—(See body mechanics.)

Glossary of Terms

mental attributes—The various cognitive qualities that enhance your fighting skills.

mental component—One of the three vital components of the CFA system. The mental component includes the cerebral aspects of fighting including the killer instinct, strategic and tactical development, analysis and integration, philosophy, and cognitive development. See physical component and spiritual component.

mesomorph—One of the three somatotypes. A body type classified by a high degree of muscularity and strength. The mesomorph possesses the ideal physique for unarmed combat. See ectomorph and endomorph.

mobility—A combative attribute. The ability to move your body quickly and freely while balanced. See footwork.

moderate response—One of the three possible counters when assaulted by a grab, choke, or hold from a standing position. Moderate response requires you to counter your opponent with a control and restraint (submission hold). See aggressive response and passive response.

modern martial art—A pragmatic combat art that has evolved to meet the demands and characteristics of the present time.

mounted position—A dominant ground-fighting position where a fighter straddles his opponent.

muscular endurance—The muscles' ability to perform the same motion or task repeatedly for a prolonged period of time.

muscular flexibility—The muscles' ability to move through maximum natural ranges.

muscular strength—The maximum force that can be exerted by a particular muscle or muscle group against resistance.

muscular/skeletal conditioning—An element of physical fitness that entails muscular strength, endurance, and flexibility.

N

naked choke—A throat choke executed from the chest to back position. This secure choke is executed with two hands and it can be performed while standing, kneeling, and ground fighting with the opponent.

neck crush – A powerful pain compliance technique used when the adversary buries his head in your chest to avoid being razed.

neutralize—See incapacitate.

neutral zone—The distance outside the kicking range at which neither the practitioner nor the assailant can touch the other.

nonaggressive physiology—Strategic body language used prior to initiating a first strike.

nontelegraphic movement—Body mechanics or movements that do not inform an assailant of your intentions.

nuclear ground-fighting tools—Specific grappling range tools designed to inflict immediate and irreversible damage. Nuclear tools and tactics include biting tactics, tearing tactics, crushing tactics, continuous choking tactics, gouging techniques, raking tactics, and all striking techniques.

O

offense—The armed and unarmed means and methods of attacking a criminal assailant.

offensive flow—Continuous offensive movements (kicks, blows, and strikes) with unbroken continuity that ultimately neutralize or terminate the opponent. See compound attack.

offensive reaction time—The elapsed time between target selection

Glossary of Terms

and target impaction.

one-mindedness—A state of deep concentration wherein you are free from all distractions (internal and external).

ostrich defense—One of the biggest mistakes one can make when defending against an opponent. This is when the practitioner looks away from that which he fears (punches, kicks, and strikes). His mentality is, "If I can't see it, it can't hurt me."

P

pain tolerance—Your ability to physically and psychologically withstand pain.

panic—The second stage of fear; overpowering fear. See fright and terror.

parry—A defensive technique: a quick, forceful slap that redirects an assailant's linear attack. There are two types of parries: horizontal and vertical.

passive response—One of the three possible counters when assaulted by a grab, choke, or hold from a standing position. Passive response requires you to nullify the assault without injuring your adversary. See aggressive response and moderate response.

patience—A combative attribute. The ability to endure and tolerate difficulty.

perception—Interpretation of vital information acquired from your senses when faced with a potentially threatening situation.

philosophical resolution—The act of analyzing and answering various questions concerning the use of violence in defense of yourself and others.

philosophy—One of the five aspects of CFA's mental component. A deep state of introspection whereby you methodically resolve critical questions concerning the use of force in defense of yourself or others.

physical attributes—The numerous physical qualities that enhance your combative skills and abilities.

physical component—One of the three vital components of the CFA system. The physical component includes the physical aspects of fighting, such as physical fitness, weapon/technique mastery, and combative attributes. See mental component and spiritual component.

physical conditioning—See combative fitness.

physical fitness—See combative fitness.

positional asphyxia—The arrangement, placement, or positioning of your opponent's body in such a way as to interrupt your breathing and cause unconsciousness or possibly death.

positioning—The spatial relationship of the assailant to the assailed person in terms of target exposure, escape, angle of attack, and various other strategic considerations.

postal attack - see going postal.

power—A physical attribute of armed and unarmed combat. The amount of force you can generate when striking an anatomical target.

power generators—Specific points on your body that generate impact power. There are three anatomical power generators: shoulders, hips, and feet.

precision—See accuracy.

preemptive strike—See first strike.

premise—An axiom, concept, rule, or any other valid reason to modify or go beyond that which has been established.

preparedness—A state of being ready for combat. There are three components of preparedness: affective preparedness, cognitive preparedness, and psychomotor preparedness.

Glossary of Terms

probable reaction dynamics - The opponent's anticipated or predicted movements or actions during both armed and unarmed combat.

proficiency training—A CFA training methodology requiring the practitioner to execute a specific body weapon, technique, maneuver, or tactic over and over for a prescribed number of repetitions. See conditioning training and street training.

proxemics—The study of the nature and effect of man's personal space.

proximity—The ability to maintain a strategically safe distance from a threatening individual.

pseudospeciation—A combative attribute. The tendency to assign subhuman and inferior qualities to a threatening assailant.

psychological conditioning—The process of conditioning the mind for the horrors and rigors of real combat.

psychomotor preparedness—One of the three components of preparedness. Psychomotor preparedness means possessing all of the physical skills and attributes necessary to defeat a formidable adversary. See affective preparedness and cognitive preparedness.

punch—A quick, forceful strike of the fists.

punching range—One of the three ranges of unarmed combat. Punching range is the mid range of unarmed combat from which the fighter uses his hands to strike his assailant. See kicking range and grappling range.

punching-range tools—The various body weapons that are employed in the punching range of unarmed combat, including finger jabs, palm-heel strikes, rear cross, knife-hand strikes, horizontal and shovel hooks, uppercuts, and hammer-fist strikes. See grappling-range tools and kicking-range tools.

Q

qualities of combat—See attributes of combat.

quarter beat - One of the four beat classifications of the Widow Maker Program. Quarter beat strikes never break contact with the assailant's face. Quarter beat strikes are primarily responsible for creating the psychological panic and trauma when Razing.

R

range—The spatial relationship between a fighter and a threatening assailant.

range deficiency—The inability to effectively fight and defend in all ranges of combat (armed and unarmed).

range manipulation—A combative attribute. The strategic manipulation of combat ranges.

range proficiency—A combative attribute. The ability to effectively fight and defend in all ranges of combat (armed and unarmed).

ranges of engagement—See combat ranges.

ranges of unarmed combat—The three distances (kicking range, punching range, and grappling range) a fighter might physically engage with an assailant while involved in unarmed combat.

raze - To level, demolish or obliterate.

razer - One who performs the Razing methodology.

razing - The second phase of the Widow Maker Program. A series of vicious close quarter techniques designed to physically and psychologically extirpate a criminal attacker.

reaction dynamics—see probable reaction dynamics.

Glossary of Terms

reaction time—The elapsed time between a stimulus and the response to that particular stimulus. See offensive reaction time and defensive reaction time.

rear cross—A straight punch delivered from the rear hand that crosses from right to left (if in a left stance) or left to right (if in a right stance).

rear side—The side of the body furthest from the assailant. See lead side.

reasonable force—That degree of force which is not excessive for a particular event and which is appropriate in protecting yourself or others.

refinement—The strategic and methodical process of improving or perfecting.

relocation principle—Also known as relocating, this is a street-fighting tactic that requires you to immediately move to a new location (usually by flanking your adversary) after delivering a compound attack.

repetition—Performing a single movement, exercise, strike, or action continuously for a specific period.

research—A scientific investigation or inquiry.

rhythm—Movements characterized by the natural ebb and flow of related elements.

ritual-oriented training—Formalized training that is conducted without intrinsic purpose. See combat-oriented training and sport-oriented training.

S

safety—One of the three criteria for a CFA body weapon, technique, maneuver, or tactic. It means that the tool, technique,

The Heavy Bag Bible

maneuver or tactic provides the least amount of danger and risk for the practitioner. See efficiency and effectiveness.

scissors hold—See guard position.

scorching – Quickly and inconspicuously applying oleoresin capsicum (hot pepper extract) on your fingertips and then razing your adversary.

self-awareness—One of the three categories of CFA awareness. Knowing and understanding yourself. This includes aspects of yourself which may provoke criminal violence and which will promote a proper and strong reaction to an attack. See criminal awareness and situational awareness.

self-confidence—Having trust and faith in yourself.

self-enlightenment—The state of knowing your capabilities, limitations, character traits, feelings, general attributes, and motivations. See self-awareness.

set—A term used to describe a grouping of repetitions.

shadow fighting—A CFA training exercise used to develop and refine your tools, techniques, and attributes of armed and unarmed combat.

sharking – A counter attack technique that is used when your adversary grabs your razing hand.

shielding wedge - a defensive maneuver used to counter an unarmed postal attack.

situational awareness—One of the three categories of CFA awareness. A state of being totally alert to your immediate surroundings, including people, places, objects, and actions. (See criminal awareness and self-awareness.)

skeletal alignment—The proper alignment or arrangement of your body. Skeletal alignment maximizes the structural integrity of striking

Glossary of Terms

tools.

skills—One of the three factors that determine who will win a street fight. Skills refers to psychomotor proficiency with the tools and techniques of combat. See Attitude and Knowledge.

slipping—A defensive maneuver that permits you to avoid an assailant's linear blow without stepping out of range. Slipping can be accomplished by quickly snapping the head and upper torso sideways (right or left) to avoid the blow.

snap back—A defensive maneuver that permits you to avoid an assailant's linear and circular blows without stepping out of range. The snap back can be accomplished by quickly snapping the head backward to avoid the assailant's blow.

somatotypes—A method of classifying human body types or builds into three different categories: endomorph, mesomorph, and ectomorph. See endomorph, mesomorph, and ectomorph.

sparring—A training exercise where two or more fighters fight each other while wearing protective equipment.

speed—A physical attribute of armed and unarmed combat. The rate or a measure of the rapid rate of motion.

spiritual component—One of the three vital components of the CFA system. The spiritual component includes the metaphysical issues and aspects of existence. See physical component and mental component.

sport-oriented training—Training that is geared for competition and governed by a set of rules. See combat-oriented training and ritual-oriented training.

sprawling—A grappling technique used to counter a double- or single-leg takedown.

square off—To be face-to-face with a hostile or threatening

assailant who is about to attack you.

stance—One of the many strategic postures you assume prior to or during armed or unarmed combat.

stick fighting—Fighting that takes place with either one or two sticks.

strategic positioning—Tactically positioning yourself to either escape, move behind a barrier, or use a makeshift weapon.

strategic/tactical development—One of the five elements of CFA's mental component.

strategy—A carefully planned method of achieving your goal of engaging an assailant under advantageous conditions.

street fight—A spontaneous and violent confrontation between two or more individuals wherein no rules apply.

street fighter—An unorthodox combatant who has no formal training. His combative skills and tactics are usually developed in the street by the process of trial and error.

street training—A CFA training methodology requiring the practitioner to deliver explosive compound attacks for 10 to 20 seconds. See condition ng training and proficiency training.

strength training—The process of developing muscular strength through systematic application of progressive resistance.

striking art—A combat art that relies predominantly on striking techniques to neutralize or terminate a criminal attacker.

striking shield—A rectangular shield constructed of foam and vinyl used to develop power in your kicks, punches, and strikes.

striking tool—A natural body weapon that impacts with the assailant's anatomical target.

strong side—The strongest and most coordinated side of your

Glossary of Terms

body.

structure—A definite and organized pattern.

style—The distinct manner in which a fighter executes or performs his combat skills.

stylistic integration—The purposeful and scientific collection of tools and techniques from various disciplines, which are strategically integrated and dramatically altered to meet three essential criteria: efficiency, effectiveness, and combative safety.

submission holds—Also known as control and restraint techniques, many of these locks and holds create sufficient pain to cause the adversary to submit.

system—The unification of principles, philosophies, rules, strategies, methodologies, tools, and techniques of a particular method of combat.

T

tactic—The skill of using the available means to achieve an end.

target awareness—A combative attribute that encompasses five strategic principles: target orientation, target recognition, target selection, target impaction, and target exploitation.

target exploitation—A combative attribute. The strategic maximization of your assailant's reaction dynamics during a fight. Target exploitation can be applied in both armed and unarmed encounters.

target impaction—The successful striking of the appropriate anatomical target.

target orientation—A combative attribute. Having a workable knowledge of the assailant's anatomical targets.

target recognition—The ability to immediately recognize appropriate anatomical targets during an emergency self-defense situation.

target selection—The process of mentally selecting the appropriate anatomical target for your self-defense situation. This is predicated on certain factors, including proper force response, assailant's positioning, and range.

target stare—A form of telegraphing in which you stare at the anatomical target you intend to strike.

target zones—The three areas in which an assailant's anatomical targets are located. (See zone one, zone two and zone three.)

technique—A systematic procedure by which a task is accomplished.

telegraphic cognizance—A combative attribute. The ability to recognize both verbal and non-verbal signs of aggression or assault.

telegraphing—Unintentionally making your intentions known to your adversary.

tempo—The speed or rate at which you speak.

terminate—To kill.

terror—The third stage of fear; defined as overpowering fear. See fright and panic.

timing—A physical and mental attribute of armed and unarmed combat. Your ability to execute a movement at the optimum moment.

tone—The overall quality or character of your voice.

tool—See body weapon.

traditional martial arts—Any martial art that fails to evolve and change to meet the demands and characteristics of its present environment.

Glossary of Terms

traditional style/system—See traditional martial arts.

training drills—The various exercises and drills aimed at perfecting combat skills, attributes, and tactics.

trap and tuck – A counter move technique used when the adversary attempts to raze you during your quarter beat assault.

U

unified mind—A mind free and clear of distractions and focused on the combative situation.

use of force response—A combative attribute. Selecting the appropriate level of force for a particular emergency self-defense situation.

V

viciousness—A combative attribute. The propensity to be extremely violent and destructive often characterized by intense savagery.

violence—The intentional utilization of physical force to coerce, injure, cripple, or kill.

visualization—Also known as mental visualization or mental imagery. The purposeful formation of mental images and scenarios in the mind's eye.

W

warm-up—A series of mild exercises, stretches, and movements designed to prepare you for more intense exercise.

weak side—The weaker and more uncoordinated side of your body.

weapon and technique mastery—A component of CFA's physical component. The kinesthetic and psychomotor development of a

The Heavy Bag Bible

weapon or combative technique.

weapon capability—An assailant's ability to use and attack with a particular weapon.

webbing - The first phase of the Widow Maker Program. Webbing is a two hand strike delivered to the assailant's chin. It is called Webbing because your hands resemble a large web that wraps around the enemy's face.

widow maker – One who makes widows by destroying husbands.

widow maker program – A CFA combat program specifically designed to teach the law abiding citizen how to use extreme force when faced with immediate threat of unlawful deadly criminal attack. The Widow Maker program is divided into two phases or methodologies: Webbing and Razing.

Y

yell—A loud and aggressive scream or shout used for various strategic reasons.

Z

zero beat – One of the four beat classifications of the Widow Maker, Feral Fighting and Savage Street Fighting Programs. Zero beat strikes are full pressure techniques applied to a specific target until it completely ruptures. They include gouging, crushing, biting, and choking techniques.

zone one—Anatomical targets related to your senses, including the eyes, temple, nose, chin, and back of neck.

zone three—Anatomical targets related to your mobility, including thighs, knees, shins, and instep.

zone two—Anatomical targets related to your breathing, including front of neck, solar plexus, ribs, and groin.

Photo Credits

Page 241: *Andre Ward begins his bag-work routine during a workout on Oct. 19 in Laurel. In preparation for his fight, Ward went for six, four-minute rounds with the bag during his daily training. (Photo by Jen Rynda) Permission granted.*

About Sammy Franco

With over 30 years of experience, Sammy Franco is one of the world's foremost authorities on armed and unarmed self-defense. Highly regarded as a leading innovator in combat sciences, Mr. Franco was one of the premier pioneers in the field of "reality-based" self-defense and martial arts instruction.

Sammy Franco is perhaps best known as the founder and creator of Contemporary Fighting Arts (CFA), a state-of-the-art offensive-based combat system that is specifically designed for real-world self-defense. CFA is a sophisticated and practical system of self-defense, designed specifically to provide efficient and effective methods to avoid, defuse, confront, and neutralize both armed and unarmed attackers.

Sammy Franco has frequently been featured in martial art magazines, newspapers, and appeared on numerous radio and television programs. Mr. Franco has also authored numerous books, magazine articles, and editorials, and has developed a popular library of instructional videos.

Sammy Franco's experience and credibility in the combat science is unequaled. One of his many accomplishments in this field includes the fact that he has earned the ranking of a Law Enforcement Master Instructor, and has designed, implemented, and taught officer survival training to the United States Border Patrol (USBP). He has instructed members of the US Secret Service, Military Special Forces, Washington DC Police Department, Montgomery County, Maryland Deputy

The Heavy Bag Bible

Sheriffs, and the US Library of Congress Police. Sammy Franco is also a member of the prestigious International Law Enforcement Educators and Trainers Association (ILEETA) as well as the American Society of Law Enforcement Trainers (ASLET) and he is listed in the "Who's Who Director of Law Enforcement Instructors."

Sammy Franco is a nationally certified Law Enforcement Instructor in the following curricula: PR-24 Side-Handle Baton, Police Arrest and Control Procedures, Police Personal Weapons Tactics, Police Power Handcuffing Methods, Police Oleoresin Capsicum Aerosol Training (OCAT), Police Weapon Retention and Disarming Methods, Police Edged Weapon Countermeasures and "Use of Force" Assessment and Response Methods.

Mr. Franco holds a Bachelor of Arts degree in Criminal Justice from the University of Maryland. He is a regularly featured speaker at a number of professional conferences and conducts dynamic and enlightening seminars on numerous aspects of self-defense and combat training.

On a personal level, Sammy Franco is an animal lover, who will go to great lengths to assist and rescue animals. Throughout the years, he's rescued everything from turkey vultures to goats. However, his most treasured moments are always spent with his beloved German Shepherd dogs.

For more information about Mr. Franco and his unique Contemporary Fighting Arts system, you can visit his website at: **SammyFranco.com** or follow him on Twitter **@RealSammyFranco**

Other Books by Sammy Franco

DOUBLE END BAG WORKOUT
For Boxing, Mixed Martial Arts & Self-Defense
by Sammy Franco

With over 200 detailed photographs, clear illustrations, and easy-to-follow instructions, Double End Bag Workout: For Boxing, Mixed Martial Arts and Self-Defense has everything you need to start training immediately. Double End Bag Workout also has beginner, intermediate and advanced workout routines that improve your speed, timing, accuracy, attack rhythm, and endurance. Whether you're an elite fighter or a complete beginner, this comprehensive book will take your boxing workout to the next level and beyond! 8.5 x 5.5, paperback, photos, illus, 260 pages.

THE COMPLETE BODY OPPONENT BAG BOOK
by Sammy Franco

In this one-of-a-kind book, Sammy Franco teaches you the many hidden training features of the body opponent bag that will improve your fighting skills and boost your conditioning. With detailed photographs, step-by-step instructions, and dozens of unique workout routines, The Complete Body Opponent Bag Book is the authoritative resource for mastering this lifelike punching bag. It covers stances, punching, kicking, grappling techniques, mobility and footwork, targets, fighting ranges, training gear, time based workouts, punching and kicking combinations, weapons training, grappling drills, ground fighting, and dozens of workouts. 8.5 x 5.5, paperback, 139 photos, illustrations, 206 pages.

THE BIGGER THEY ARE, THE HARDER THEY FALL
How to Fight a Bigger and Stronger Opponent in the Street
by Sammy Franco

Sammy Franco was concerned that no book on the market successfully tackled the specific problem of fighting a larger, stronger opponent. In The Bigger They Are, The Harder They Fall, he addresses that all-important issue and delivers the solid information you'll need to win a street fight when the odds seem stacked against you. In this one-of-a-kind book, Sammy Franco prepares you both mentally and physically for the fight of your life. Unless you're a lineman for the NFL, there may come a day when you will face an opponent who can dominate you through sheer mass and power. Read and study this book before that day comes. 8.5 x 5.5, paperback, photos, illus, 212 pages.

UNLEASH HELL
A Step-By-Step Guide to Devastating Widow Maker Combinations
by Sammy Franco

Unleash Hell is the third installment in the best-selling Widow Maker program book series. It takes you beyond the initial Widow Maker program by teaching you Franco's favorite fight-stopping Widow Maker techniques that will overwhelm and destroy your opponent in a matter of seconds. This unique program enables you to burn devastating Widow Maker combinations into muscle memory while systematically developing extraordinary fighting hand speed. Unleash Hell also includes advanced Widow Maker fighting concepts such as hand-held weapon integration, razing amplifiers, environmental exploitation tactics, and traumatic schematics. 8.5 x 5.5, paperback, photos, illus, 216 pages.

THE WIDOW MAKER PROGRAM
Extreme Self-Defense for Deadly Force Situations
by Sammy Franco

The Widow Maker Program is a shocking and revolutionary fighting style designed to unleash extreme force when faced with the immediate threat of an unlawful deadly criminal attack. In this unique book, self-defense innovator Sammy Franco teaches you his brutal and unorthodox combat style that is virtually indefensible and utterly devastating. With over 250 photographs and detailed step-by-step instructions, The Widow Maker Program teaches you Franco's surreptitious Webbing and Razing techniques. When combined, these two fighting methods create an unstoppable force capable of destroying the toughest adversary. 8.5 x 5.5, paperback, photos, illus, 218 pages.

FERAL FIGHTING
Advanced Widow Maker Fighting Techniques
by Sammy Franco

In this sequel, Sammy Franco marches forward with cutting-edge concepts and techniques that will take your self-defense skills to entirely new levels of combat performance. Feral Fighting includes Franco's revolutionary Shielding Wedge technique. When used correctly, it transforms you into an unstoppable human meat grinder, capable of destroying any criminal adversary. Feral Fighting also teaches you the cunning art or Scorching. Learn how to convert your fingertips into burning torches that generate over 2 million scoville heat units causing excruciating pain and temporarily blindness. 8.5 x 5.5, paperback, photos, illustrations, 204 pages.

MAXIMUM DAMAGE
Hidden Secrets Behind Brutal Fighting Combination
by Sammy Franco

Maximum Damage teaches you the quickest ways to beat your opponent in the street by exploiting his physical and psychological reactions in a fight. Learn how to stay two steps ahead of your adversary by knowing exactly how he will react to your strikes before they are delivered. In this unique book, reality based self-defense expert Sammy Franco reveals his unique Probable Reaction Dynamic (PRD) fighting method. Probable reaction dynamics are both a scientific and comprehensive offensive strategy based on the positional theory of combat. Regardless of your style of fighting, PRD training will help you overpower your opponent by seamlessly integrating your strikes into brutal fighting combinations that are fast, ferocious and final! 8.5 x 5.5, paperback, 240 photos, illustrations, 238 pages.

SAVAGE STREET FIGHTING
Tactical Savagery as a Last Resort
by Sammy Franco

In this revolutionary book, Sammy Franco reveals the science behind his most primal street fighting method. Savage Street Fighting is a brutal self-defense system specifically designed to teach the law-abiding citizen how to use "Tactical Savagery" when faced with the immediate threat of an unlawful deadly criminal attack. Savage Street Fighting is systematically engineered to protect you when there are no other self-defense options left! With over 300 photographs and detailed step-by-step instructions, Savage Street Fighting is a must-have book for anyone concerned about real world self-defense. Now is the time to learn how to unleash your inner beast! 8.5 x 5.5, paperback, 317 photos, illustrations, 232 pages.

FIRST STRIKE
End a Fight in Ten Seconds or Less!
by Sammy Franco

Learn how to stop any attack before it starts by mastering the art of the preemptive strike. First Strike gives you an easy-to-learn yet highly effective self-defense game plan for handling violent close-quarter combat encounters. First Strike will teach you instinctive, practical and realistic self-defense techniques that will drop any criminal attacker to the floor with one punishing blow. By reading this book and by practicing, you will learn the hard-hitting skills necessary to execute a punishing first strike and ultimately prevail in a self-defense situation. 8.5 x 5.5, paperback, photos, illustrations, 202 pages.

WAR MACHINE
How to Transform Yourself Into A Vicious & Deadly Street Fighter
by Sammy Franco

War Machine is a book that will change you for the rest of your life! When followed accordingly, War Machine will forge your mind, body and spirit into iron. Once armed with the mental and physical attributes of the War Machine, you will become a strong and confident warrior that can handle just about anything that life may throw your way. In essence, War Machine is a way of life. Powerful, intense, and hard. 11 x 8.5, paperback, photos, illustrations, 210 pages.

INVINCIBLE
Mental Toughness Techniques for Peak Performance
by Sammy Franco

Invincible is a treasure trove of battle-tested techniques and strategies for improving mental toughness in all aspects of life. It teaches you how to unlock the true power of your mind and achieve success in sports, fitness, high-risk professions, self-defense, and other peak performance activities. However, you don't have to be an athlete or warrior to benefit from this unique mental toughness book. In fact, the mental skills featured in this indispensable program can be used by anyone who wants to reach their full potential in life. 8.5 x 5.5, paperback, photos, illus, 250 pages

CONTEMPORARY FIGHTING ARTS, LLC
"Real World Self-Defense Since 1989"
SammyFranco.com

Printed in Great Britain
by Amazon